Lightroom Classic? 2nd Edition

The Quickest Ways to Do the
Things You Want to Do, Right Now!

Scott Kelby

Author of the top-selling digital photography
book, ever—*The Digital Photography Book*, part 1

How Do I Do That In Lightroom Classic? 2nd Edition

The *How Do I Do That in Lightroom Classic Book* **Team**

MANAGING EDITOR
Kim Doty

TECHNICAL EDITOR
Cindy Snyder

COPY EDITOR
Sarah Freeman

ART DIRECTOR
Jessica Maldonado

PHOTOGRAPHY
Scott Kelby

PUBLISHED BY

Rocky Nook

Rocky Nook, Inc.
1010 B Street, Suite 350
San Rafael, CA 94901

Composed in Univers and Avenir (Linotype) by KelbyOne.

Trademarks
All terms mentioned in this book that are known to be trademarks or service marks have been appropriately capitalized. Rocky Nook cannot attest to the accuracy of this information. Use of a term in the book should not be regarded as affecting the validity of any trademark or service mark.

Photoshop and Lightroom are registered trademarks of Adobe Systems Incorporated.

Warning and Disclaimer
This book is designed to provide information about Lightroom. Every effort has been made to make this book as complete and as accurate as possible, but no warranty of fitness is implied.

The information is provided on an as-is basis. The author and Rocky Nook shall have neither the liability nor responsibility to any person or entity with respect to any loss or damages arising from the information contained in this book or from the use of the discs or programs that may accompany it.

THIS PRODUCT IS NOT ENDORSED OR SPONSORED BY ADOBE SYSTEMS INCORPORATED, PUBLISHER OF ADOBE PHOTOSHOP, PHOTOSHOP ELEMENTS, AND PHOTOSHOP LIGHTROOM.

ISBN: 978-1-68198-420-9

10 9 8 7 6 5 4 3 2 1

Printed and bound in Canada
Distributed in the US by Ingram Publisher Services
Distributed in the UK and Europe by Publishers Group UK

Library of Congress Control Number: 2018950883

www.kelbyone.com
www.rockynook.com

*This book is dedicated
to my wife Kalebra
for putting the stars in
my sky, the song in my heart,
and the smile on my face each
and every day. I love you madly!*

Acknowledgments

Although only one name appears on the spine of this book, it takes a team of dedicated and talented people to pull a project like this together. I'm not only delighted to be working with them, but I also get the honor and privilege of thanking them here.

To my amazing wife Kalebra: You continue to reinforce what everybody always tells me— I'm the luckiest guy in the world.

To my son Jordan: If there's a dad more proud of his son than I am, I've yet to meet him. You are just a wall of awesome! So proud of the fine young man you've become.

To my beautiful daughter Kira: You are a little clone of your mom, and that's the best compliment I could ever give you.

To my big brother Jeff: Your boundless generosity, kindness, positive attitude, and humility have been an inspiration to me my entire life, and I'm just so honored to be your brother.

To my editor Kim Doty: I feel incredibly fortunate to have you as my editor on these books. In fact, I can't imagine doing them without you. You truly are a joy to work with.

To my book designer Jessica Maldonado: I love the way you design, and all the clever little things you add to everything you do. Our book team struck gold when we found you!

To my tech editor Cindy Snyder: I feel very blessed to have you still working with us on these books. Thank you, Cindy!

To my dear friend and sounding board Erik Kuna: Thanks for putting all the kittens back in the box while I'm off in "book land," and thanks for all your vision, heart, insight, advice, and friendship. 3...2...1...Liftoff!

To my dear friend and business partner Jean A. Kendra: Thanks for putting up with me all these years, and for your support for all my crazy ideas. It really means a lot.

To my assistant Jeanne Jilleba: Thanks for constantly putting my wheels back on the track. I'm very grateful to have your help, your talent, and your immeasurable patience every day.

To Ted Waitt, my awesome "Editor for life" at Rocky Nook: Thank you for having faith in my crazy ideas, and for helping me work through the rough ones, so we come out with awesome books on the other end.

To my publisher Scott Cowlin: I'm so delighted I still get to work with you, and for your open mind and willingness to try new things, open new doors, and explore lots of "what-ifs."

To my mentors John Graden, Jack Lee, Dave Gales, Judy Farmer, and Douglas Poole: Thank you for your wisdom and whip-cracking—they have helped me immeasurably.

Most importantly, I want to thank God, and His Son Jesus Christ, for leading me to the woman of my dreams, for blessing us with such amazing children, for allowing me to make a living doing something I truly love, for always being there when I need Him, for blessing me with a wonderful, fulfilling, and happy life, and such a warm, loving family to share it with.

Scott is Editor and Publisher of *Lightroom Magazine*; producer of LightroomKillerTips.com; Editor and co-founder of *Photoshop User* magazine; host of *The Grid*, the influential, live, weekly talk show for photographers; and is founder of the annual Scott Kelby's Worldwide Photo Walk.®

He is President and CEO of KelbyOne, an online educational community for learning Lightroom, Photoshop, and photography.

Scott is a photographer, designer, and award-winning author of more than 90 books, including *The Adobe Photoshop Lightroom Book for Digital Photographers*; *Light It, Shoot It, Retouch It: Learn Step by Step How to Go from Empty Studio to Finished Image*; *The Adobe Photoshop Book for Digital Photographers*; *Professional Portrait Retouching Techniques for Photographers Using Photoshop*; and *The Digital Photography Book* series. The first book in the series, *The Digital Photography Book*, part 1, has become the top-selling book on digital photography in history.

For six years in a row, Scott has been honored with the distinction of being the world's #1 best-selling author of photography techniques books. His books have been translated into dozens of different languages, including Chinese, Russian, Spanish, Korean, Polish, Taiwanese, French, German, Italian, Japanese, Hebrew, Dutch, Swedish, Turkish, and Portuguese, among many others. He is recipient of the prestigious ASP International Award, presented annually by the American Society of Photographers for "…contributions in a special or significant way to the ideals of Professional Photography as an art and a science," and the HIPA award, presented for his contributions to photography education worldwide.

Scott is Conference Technical Chair for the annual Photoshop World Conference and a frequent speaker at conferences and trade shows around the world. He is featured in a series of online learning courses at KelbyOne.com and has been training Photoshop users and photographers since 1993.

For more information on Scott, visit:

His daily Lightroom blog: **lightroomkillertips.com**

His personal blog: **scottkelby.com**

Twitter: **@scottkelby**

Facebook: **facebook.com/skelby**

Instagram: **@scottkelby**

Google+: **+ScottKelby**

Table of Contents

Table of Contents

Chapter 3   61

How to Customize Lightroom
How to Make It Work Like You Want It to Work

Table of Contents

Chapter 4   **75**

How to Edit Your Images
Develop Module Stuff

Table of Contents

Chapter 5   111
How to Use the Brushes
The Adjustment Brush, the Spot Removal Brush, and All That Stuff

Chapter 6   137
How to Create Special Effects
The Easy Way to Get Cool Looks Fast

Table of Contents

Chapter 7   153

How to Save Your Images
Using Lightroom's Export

Chapter 8   167

How to Make Photo Books
Using Lightroom's Built-In Book Module

Table of Contents

Chapter 9   193
How to Make Awesome Slide Shows
Just Don't Put Any Emphasis on the Word "Awesome"

Chapter 10   213
How to Print
Working in the Print Module

Table of Contents

Chapter 11   239
How to Use Lightroom on Your Mobile Device
It's Lightroom on the Road

Table of Contents

Chapter 12   273
Other Stuff You'll Want to Know
All That Other Stuff? It's in This Chapter

If You Skip This One Page, You'll Regret It for...

(1) Okay, it's possible that I exaggerated a bit in that headline...as a ruse to get you to read this quick intro, but only because it's for your own good. Well, technically it's for both our goods (goods?), because if you skip this, you might not totally grock (grock?) how this book was designed to be used, which is different than most other books for a number of reasons, the first being most other books don't try to trick you into reading the intro. But, in this case, I had to do it (and I feel semi-bad about it, sort of, kinda, in a way), because (a) I want you to get the most out of this book (another selfish author only wanting for himself), and (b) you want you to get the most out of it (you paid for it, or at the very least, shoplifted it), so it's for both our goods (thankfully, my editor doesn't require me to use real words). Anyway, in short, here's how to use this book:

Don't read it in order. It's not that kind of book. This is more like an "I'm stuck. I need help right now" book, so when you're working in Lightroom and need to know how to do a particular thing right this very minute, you just pick it up, turn to the chapter where it would be (Print, Slideshow, Organizing, Importing, etc.), find the thing you need to do, and I tell you exactly how to do it, pretty succinctly ($5 word—bonus points!), and you're off and running back in Lightroom. If I did my job right, you should only be in this book for like a minute at a time—just long enough to learn that one important thing you need now, and then you're back to lounging on your yacht (at least, that's how I imagine your life will roll after buying this book).

Same Thing Over Here. Regret (or Worse). Ack!

(2) There's something in here that, depending on your general disposition, might make you mad. Well, maddish. This is my fourth book with the awesome folks at Rocky Nook, so I might be reaching a new audience (perhaps this is the first book of mine you've purchased, but I hope that's not the case because my son is going to an out-of-state college, and it's crazy expensive, so it'd really help with his tuition if you bought, I dunno, at least six or 22 of my previous books). Anyway, I do this thing that either delights readers or makes them spontaneously burst into flames of anger, but it has been a tradition, so now it's a "thing" I can't get out of: how I write the chapter intros. In a normal book, they would give you some insight into what's coming in the chapter. But, mine…um…well, they don't. Honestly, they have little, if anything, to do with what's in the chapter, as I've designed them to simply be a "mental break" between chapters, and these quirky, rambling intros have become a trademark of mine. Luckily, I've delegated the "crazy stuff" to just those intro pages—the rest of the book is pretty regular, with me telling you how to do things just like I would tell a friend sitting beside me. But, I had to warn you about these, just in case you're a Mr. Grumpypants and all serious. If that sounds like you, I'm begging you, please skip the chapter intros—they'll just get on your nerves, and then you'll write me a letter to tell me how the book was "unreadable" because of those few pages, and you'll mention my mother, my upbringing, etc. So, read them at your own risk. Okay, that's pretty much it. You're now fully certified and crosschecked (flight attendant lingo) to use this book and I really hope you find it helpful in your Lightroom journey.

Chapter 1

How to Get Your Images Into Lightroom

The Importing Process

This is the fourth book I've written that's published by the fine folks at Rocky Nook and, because of that, I think it's only fair that I warn you once again about something that is a long-standing tradition of mine, and that is to write chapter intros that have little or nothing to do with what's actually in the chapter. I want you to think of these as a "mental break" between chapters and not something that actually adds any value to the book, or to your life, whatsoever. To balance this, I try to put an interesting picture on the facing page—it helps give it some legitimacy—but (a) the picture isn't always interesting and (b) it hasn't ever helped the legitimacy so far. Why this is important (it isn't, by the way) is that I really want you to get a lot out of this book and reading these chapter openers is, honestly, a step in the wrong direction. Look, I just want to be straight with you: these chapter openers are a trap. They snare you and, before you know it, you're turning to other chapters because you can't believe the other openers are as sophomoric and shallow as this one, but then you realize they have each drained a little more out of the pool. So, you keep reading one after another, instead of learning about Lightroom, because you're wondering how my publisher lets me get away with this, and you're either laughing or crying, because on some level you paid for these pages, and you either think "That's okay, I dig this stuff," or you're thinking, "Scott must die!" If you're thinking the latter, please don't write me a Mr. Grumpypants letter that starts with "Mr. Kelby" (nobody calls me Mr. Kelby outside of the occasional federal court judge or the guards, but they usually just use my inmate number) because I'm obliged (through a sworn oath of chastity and pestilence between authors) to turn the letter over to my publisher, who I'm certain will make it poster-sized, put it on their wall, and dance around it saying lurid incantations until my contract with them has expired. Yes, that's how it goes down at Rocky Nook.

How Do I... Make Lightroom Open Automatically When I Insert a Memory Card?

Go to Lightroom's Preferences (under the Lightroom [PC: Edit] menu), click on the General tab, and you'll see Show Import Dialog When a Memory Card Is Detected in the Import Options section. Turn that checkbox on, and you're all set.

There are four choices, and the one that will make your thumbnails appear the fastest is to choose **Minimal** from the Build Previews pop-up menu, at the top of the File Handling panel (in the top right of the Import window). It just grabs the small preview that your camera has already created, so it doesn't have to do a lot of rendering—it just shows that thumbnail lickity-split (I always choose Minimal myself, because I have a severe lack of patience).

This is a two-parter, because it starts with you creating a metadata template with your copyright info (you do this before you even open the Import window and luckily you just have to do this once). In the Library module, go under the Metadata menu (up at the top of the screen) and choose **Edit Metadata Presets** to bring up the Edit Metadata Presets dialog (shown above left). Just type in all your copyright info, then from the Preset pop-up menu, choose **Save Current Settings as New Preset**, and give your preset a name (I named mine, "Scott's Copyright." You should probably choose a different name. Just sayin'). Click the Done button and part one is done (again, you only have to do this once. Well, technically, once a year so your copyright year is up-to-date, but you know what I mean). The second part is simple: when you're in the Import window, go to the Apply During Import panel on the right side of the window, and from the Metadata pop-up menu, choose the preset you saved in part one (as shown above on the right). Okay, that's it. Now, when the current batch of images is imported, they will have your copyright info embedded into each image. Each time you import, you can choose whether you want to include your copyright.

How Do I... Speed Things Up by Making a Preset?

If you use the same Import settings again and again, there's no sense in inputting them every time from scratch, so make a preset. Open the Import window **(Command-Shift-I [PC: Ctrl-Shift-I])** and enter all your favorite settings. Then, at the bottom center of the window, choose **Save Current Settings as New Preset** from the Import Preset pop-up menu (as shown above). Now, whenever you open the Import window, you can choose any of the presets you've made (here, I've made one that converts the images to black and white on import, one for automatically backing up the images to a second attached drive, one that includes smart previews, and then one with my regular old everyday settings).

How Do I... Apply Smart Previews? (And Why Should I?)

So, why would you want a smart preview in the first place? It's mostly for two groups of users: (1) You work on a laptop and don't have a ton of hard drive space, so you use an external hard drive to store your high-resolution images. But, when you travel and disconnect that hard drive, you can't edit your photos in the Develop module because they're just small thumbnail previews, and Lightroom won't let you edit low-res junk. A smart preview is a larger preview, but specially compressed so it doesn't take up much room on your hard drive (only around 1MB apiece). These smart previews can be edited in the Develop module (cropped and everything), just like you had the high-res version there (they can even be printed up to a certain size). When you reconnect your hard drive, it updates the high-res images with all the changes you made to the smart previews (pretty smart, eh?). (2) It's for users who work with Lightroom on their mobile devices (it uses these smart previews to do its thing). Luckily, creating smart previews on import is about the easiest thing you can do: in the Import window, in the File Handling panel (in the top right), just turn on the Build Smart Previews checkbox and it will build them as they're imported (it doesn't slow things down because it builds them in the background once they're imported. You can see their progress in the Activity Center—just click directly on the Lightroom logo in the upper-left corner of the Library module).

6

If you want to have a second copy of the images you're importing, first make sure you have a second place to send them to, like an external hard drive—so, one set of images goes onto your computer or the external drive you store your images on, and the backup set goes onto that second external hard drive. Once you've got a second storage device in place, in the Import window, in the File Handling panel (in the top right), turn on the Make a Second Copy To checkbox, and then choose that external hard drive (or wherever you're going to save your second copy). Now, the images you're importing will be backed up to that second drive. I do want you to know about something that trips up a lot of folks with this process: it's backing up those images in the state they are in now—untouched, straight-out-of-the-camera (think of them as the "negatives" from the old film days). If one day you had to go to that backup copy you made, none of the stuff you're going to be doing to the images you're importing will reflect in that second backup. It's just a backup of the images right out of the camera. You may be perfectly fine with that, but I just wanted you to know now.

If you've shot a bunch of images that you already know you want to be converted to black and white, you can easily apply a black-and-white preset to them as they're imported. You do this in the Import window, in the Apply During Import panel (on the right), by clicking on the Develop Settings pop-up menu. You'll see a list of the presets that come with Lightroom (and any you create yourself, under User Presets. See Chapter 6 for more on presets). You can choose any preset you like here, not just the B&W presets (but they're a pretty popular choice to apply on import). That's all there is to it. Also, don't worry—even though you applied these on import, you can always remove the preset by hitting the Reset All button in the Library module's Quick Develop panel or the Reset button at the bottom of the Develop module's right side Panels area.

Applying generic keywords (basically, search terms) when you're importing a bunch of similar photos will make finding them later even easier. You do this in the Import window, in the Keywords field of the Apply During Import panel (on the right). Just click in this field, start typing—put a comma between each keyword or phrase—and they'll be added to each image as they're imported. Once imported, you can search for these images using any one (or more) of those keywords you added during import using Lightroom's Find feature (found under the Library menu) or Library Filter bar (above the center Preview area).

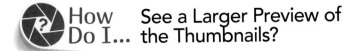

How Do I... See a Larger Preview of the Thumbnails?

There are two ways to do this in the Import window: (1) If you want to see all the thumbnails much larger, just click-and-drag the Thumbnails slider (below the bottom-right corner of the center Preview area) to the right—the farther you drag, the bigger the thumbnails. If you just want to see one image really large, double-click on it and it zooms to fill the Preview area (as seen above). Want to zoom in a little tighter? Just click once more on the zoomed-in preview and it zooms in a bit more. To return to the thumbnail Grid view, just press the letter **G** or click on the first icon below the bottom-left corner of the Preview area.

Look up in the top-right corner of the Import window. You see the word "To" in the white box? That's where your images are being copied/moved "to," and you'll see either the name of your computer, external hard drive, or if you're adding images already on your computer, you'll probably just see "My Catalog," which means your images aren't actually being moved or copied, they're just being added to your Lightroom catalog. By the way, you can see where your images are coming from, what's happening to them, and where they're going anytime by just looking from left to right at the top of the Import window. Look over at the top left. You'll see the word "From" in a white box, followed by the location where your images are now (in my case, they're on a memory card from my camera). In the top center, you'll see what's going to happen to them (notice the word "Copy" is highlighted here? That lets you know these images are going to be copied). Okay, so where are they being copied to? Again, look over at the far right where it says "To"—that's where they're going to be copied to. If you want to change where they're being copied to, just click directly on that destination (in my case, I'd click directly on the words "External Hard Drive") and choose a new destination from the pop-up menu that appears.

Only thumbnails with a checkmark at the top left of their grid cell will get imported, and by default they all have checkmarks (so, it's going to import every image). But, if there's an image you don't want imported (I don't import those that are obviously blurry, or the flash didn't fire, or are just really dumb-looking, even as a thumbnail), just turn off that checkbox. When you do this, the image dims so you can see at a glance which images won't be imported. There are also two handy buttons beneath the Preview area: Check All turns all the checkboxes back on and Uncheck All turns them all off (that's handy if you want to bring in just a few photos, instead of a whole bunch).

How Do I... Import Photos Already on My Computer?

At the top left of the Import window, in the Source panel, you can click on your computer and it displays its contents in a hierarchical list below. It basically displays all the folders on your computer, and you can just navigate to the folder of images you want to import. But, here's a shortcut that can help speed things up: First, chances are the images you want to import from your computer are in your Pictures folder, and if you want to jump right there, just click on the name of your computer's hard drive at the top left of the window (next to the word "From"). This brings up a pop-up menu with the most-likely places your pictures are saved—like your Pictures folder, or your desktop, or your Movies folder (as shown above, on the right), plus a long list of places you've recently imported pictures from (or you can choose Other Source to select a location not in the menu). Anyway, once you navigate to the folder where your images are located (using the Source panel, as shown above, on the left), just click Import and they'll come racing in (I say racing, because when they're already on your computer, and don't have to be imported from a memory card, they come in faster than a greased pig).

Chapter 2

How to Organize Your Images

Working in the Library Module

When you think about it, our parents actually had the ideal photo organization system: they stored all their photos in a shoebox. Here's why that was so brilliant: (1) Nobody could "hack" into their shoebox. Nobody was sitting in a small, dark Internet cafe in North Korea thinking of ways to crack their password to steal all their shoebox photos and distribute them on the web. (2) If they wanted to get to your parents' shoebox, they'd have to go and break into their house, but once inside, they'd see other stuff, like a TV, and a stereo, and maybe some jewelry, so they'd take those instead because if they grabbed some random shoebox and ran, there was a more than reasonable chance it would be filled with a pair of Hush Puppies (which, apparently, is all our parents wore back then. Well, at least the dads. The moms wore Penny Loafers, which were named after a character from the popular TV show *Lost in Space*—Betty Loafers). And, reason #3: Google didn't have secret access to their images, like they do today, where they have total unrestricted access to all your images (even your nude selfies), even if you never uploaded them to Google Photos. In fact, they have access to all your nude selfies, even if you've never taken one, if that gives you any idea of their power. You see, back in the 1940s and '50s, Google wasn't as powerful as they are today (where they have power akin to that of Skynet—if that sounds familiar, it's from the popular TV show *Gunsmoke*), but today we use the next best thing, which is Lightroom, but don't worry, it comes with a plug-in that, with just one click, bypasses Google altogether and sends all your family photos directly to the North Korean Internet cafe of your choice.

How Do I... Mark My Best Photos?

There are a few different ways to do this, but whichever one(s) you choose, after you apply any of them, you can ask Lightroom to just show you those that you chose. You can: (a) Press **P** to add a Pick flag, which marks an image's thumbnail with a little white flag, which lets you know you picked it as a keeper. If you make a mistake and accidentally mark one you didn't mean to, press **U** to unflag it. (b) You can add star ratings (the standard 1–5 stars) by pressing the numbers 1 through 5 on your keyboard, and it applies little black stars to the thumbnail. Or, (c) you can add color labels (go under the Photo menu, under Set Color Label), which apply a color tint to the thumbnail's border and area surrounding it. Then, you can ask Lightroom to show you any photos with a particular color label or any combination thereof (like just the ones with yellow or red labels). Plus, you can add a combination of all three to any photo (for example, an image can have a Pick flag, a star rating, and a color label). Now, how do you see just the images you like? At the top right of the Filmstrip are icons (seen above, at the bottom) that let you filter down to just your flagged, star-rated, or color-labeled photos—they're grayed out at first. To see just the photos that you flagged as Picks, click the white flag icon twice (the first time you do this, you have to click twice. After that, just click once). To see just your photos with a star rating, click-and-drag over as many stars as you want to see (e.g., drag to three stars to see just your three-star images). For labels, click on the color you want and you just see images you tagged with that color.

Just click on the photo you want to delete and press the **Delete (PC: Backspace)** key, and it removes that image (or as many images as you selected) immediately. This doesn't delete the image from Lightroom or your computer, just from that particular collection. By the way, it doesn't ask you any questions or bring up a dialog—you hit the key and it's gone! If you delete one by accident, just Undo (press **Command-Z [PC: Ctrl-Z]**).

How Do I... Zoom In to See My Images Closer?

Click on the thumbnail of the image you want to see larger, then press **Command–+** (plus sign; **PC: Ctrl–+**) and it zooms into the next magnification level up. Press that shortcut again, and it zooms in tighter. Press it again, even tighter. (*Note:* To choose how tight the final zoom is, click on the arrows at the right side of the Navigator panel's header [in the Library module's left side Panels area] to get the pop-up menu.) To zoom back out, just press **Command–-** (minus sign; **PC: Ctrl–-**).

How Do I... See What F-Stop I Shot My Photo At?

Lightroom lists any information your camera embedded in your file over in the Metadata panel in the Library module's right side Panels area. In Default view (chosen in the pop-up menu on the left side of the panel header), the information is in the bottom section and includes the f-stop and a whole bunch of other things, like your shutter speed, ISO, the lens you used, the make and model of your camera, whether your flash fired, what focal length you shot it at, the date and time you took the shot, and so on.

Lightroom Classic calls albums "collections," and to create a collection of images you like, select the images first (press-and-hold the Command [PC: Ctrl] key and click on as many images as you'd like), then you can either go over to the Collections panel (in the left side Panels area), click the + (plus sign) button on the right side of the panel header, and choose **Create Collection** to bring up the Create Collection dialog (seen above). Or, you can select your images and use the keyboard shortcut **Command-N (PC: Ctrl-N)** to bring up the same dialog. Once the dialog appears, the Include Selected Photos checkbox is already turned on for you, so all you really have to do is type in a name for this collection, click the Create button, and this new collection will appear (in alphabetical order) over in your Collections panel. To see just the images in that collection, simply click on it.

There is no "official" way to do this, but there are probably a dozen ways, so I'm going to share how I organize a big shoot like a wedding. The key here is using a collection set, which is basically one big main folder that all your individual collections go inside. For example, as soon as I'm back from a wedding, I create a collection set and name it with the name of the wedding (as seen above). Then, I go ahead and create a bunch of collection sets inside of that main set (I'll add the photos to them once I start sorting the images)—typical ones might be named: Rehearsal Dinner; Bride Getting Ready; Formals; Invites, Flowers & Details; Ceremony; Reception; Leaving the Church; and so on. Why are these collection sets? Because I'm going to need three collections inside of each. For example, inside the Bride Getting Ready collection set, you'd find three collections: (1) All (all the shots of the bride getting ready), (2) Picks (these shots have a chance of making the final wedding album), and (3) Selects (these are the very best ones from the Picks collection and are the ones that will be included in the wedding album or shared with the bride—these are the ones that get retouched, edited, and so on). Once those are in place, I import all the photos from the wedding, select big groups of images, and drag them into the appropriate collection sets. Then, I begin my process of going through the collections named "All," marking the really good ones as Picks, then I turn on the Picks filter to see just those and drag them into my Picks collections. Now I start the narrowing down process again to find the very best of the best. Those go into my Selects collections.

One of the nice things about this shortcut is that it works from anywhere, in any module you're working in within Lightroom: just press the letter **G** and it will jump you directly to the Library module and display the images you're working on as a grid of thumbnails (this is basically the "home base" of Lightroom).

If you don't see the Library Filter bar at the top of your thumbnail grid, press the backslash key (\) on your keyboard. Then, click on the collection you want it to search through in the Collections panel (or have it search all your photos in Lightroom by going to the Catalog panel near the top of the left side Panels area and clicking on All Photographs). Now that you've told Lightroom where to search, let's start searching. If you want to search by typing in a name, press **Command-F (PC: Ctrl-F)** or click on the word "Text" and a text entry field appears to its right. Just type in the word you want to search for. Any images that have that word in its name, as a keyword, or a caption, will instantly appear. If you want to search by date, then click on Metadata up in that Filter bar instead, and it will immediately display lists of search results based on the default criteria listed at the top of each of the four columns (you can choose different criteria by clicking on the name of the criterion and a huge pop-up menu of options appears). By default, Date is in the first column and it lists all the dates of images where you're searching. To see just those images from a particular year, click on the year. To narrow things down further, click on the little black arrow that appears to the left of the year, and it shows you the months in that year that you have photos from, and how many photos you have in each month. Click on any month to see just the images from that month. Click the little arrow again and you can narrow it down even further—to the particular day you took the shot. Here, you can see I quickly found the 20 images I took on Tuesday, April 3, 2018. Pretty amazing, eh?

If you see an exclamation point in a little dotted rectangle in the top-right corner of a thumbnail cell, it means Lightroom has lost the link to that original image (which means you moved the image, or its folder, or both, to a different location, or it was on an external hard drive and that hard drive isn't connected). So, just click on that little exclamation point and it brings up the warning dialog you see above, letting you know the last known location of that photo. Obviously, it's not there now or you wouldn't have this "lost original" problem, but this is easy to fix: just click the Locate button, then navigate to where the original photo actually is now, click on the image, click the Select button, and the problem's fixed. If the missing original is on an external drive, and you haven't really moved the file on that drive, the drive's just not plugged in, well…go plug it in, and problem solved.

Press-and-hold the Command key on a Mac, or the Ctrl key on a Windows PC, and click on as many photos as you'd like selected. You can do this either in Grid view or in the Filmstrip along the bottom.

There are two ways to do this, but the first way I'm going to show you I think works best because you can do this from no matter where you are in Lightroom. The second way makes you jump over to the Library module first, so my preferred method is to go down to the top-left side of the Filmstrip along the bottom, click on the path to your currently visible images (in this case, I was looking at my Previous Import), and at the top of the pop-up menu that appears, you'll see **All Photographs**. Just choose that and you're good to go. Again, the advantage of using this method is that it's always available to you in any module (Book, Print, Map, you name it). The other method is that you first switch to the Library module, then go to the Catalog panel (in the left side Panels area), and click on All Photographs there. They both work (the second one is just a little more work).

How Do I... See Just the Photos I Imported Last?

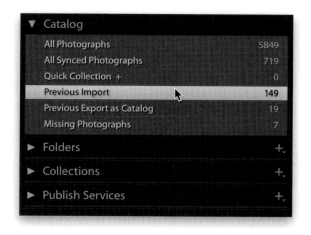

You can either use the Filmstrip pop-up menu I showed on the previous page, or go to the Catalog panel in the Library module (it's near the top of the left side Panels area) and click on **Previous Import** in either place (as seen above).

Rename 1 Photo

File Naming: Custom Name

Custom Text: Fashion Studio   Start Number:

Example: Fashion Studio.CR2   Cancel   OK

Rename 6 Photos

File Naming: Custom Name - Sequence

Custom Text: Fashion Studio   Start Number: 1

Example: Fashion Studio-1.CR2   Cancel   OK

In the Library module, select the photo (or photos) you want to rename and then go under the Library menu and choose **Rename Photos**. When the dialog appears, if you're just renaming one photo, click on the File Naming pop-up menu, choose **Custom Name,** and then type in the name you want. If you've selected multiple photos you want to rename, they can't all have the same exact name, right? So, instead, you'd choose **Custom Name – Sequence**, and then over in the Start Number field, enter the number you want the automatic file numbering to start with (this number is added after the custom name, so if you type "Fashion Studio" as your name, it will automatically add the -1, -2, -3, and so on, for as many images as you have selected).

There are three ways to do this: (1) in the Library module, go under the Photo menu and choose either **Rotate Left (CCW)** or **Rotate Right (CW)**, as shown above; (2) use the keyboard shortcut **Command-[(PC: Ctrl-[)** or **Command-] (PC: Ctrl-])**—those are the bracket keys, located just to the right of the letter P on your keyboard; or (3) in the thumbnail Grid view in the Library module, by default there are two little rotation arrows in the bottom corners of each thumbnail's cell (if you don't see them, move your cursor over the cell of the image you want to rotate and they should appear. If they still don't appear, press **Command-J [PC: Ctrl-J]** to bring up the View Options dialog and, under Compact Cells Extras, make sure the Rotation checkbox is turned on, and you should be good to go). That being said, your best bet is still the keyboard shortcuts simply because they're the fastest and they work in both the Library and Develop modules.

In the Library module, select a photo (or a bunch of photos), then go to the Keyword-ing panel (in the right side Panels area). Right below where it says "Enter Keywords" at the top of the panel is a text field. Just click your cursor once inside it and start typing in keywords (these are search terms, so add words you might actually use when searching for this image[s]). Be sure to separate each keyword with a comma. When you're done, press the Return (PC: Enter) key on your keyboard and those keywords are now embedded into your photo (or photos, if you selected more than one).

How Do I... Compare Two Photos Side by Side?

If you want to look at two similar photos side by side, just select them and then press the letter **C** on your keyboard. This puts the selected photos in Compare view, which is actually a step up from just putting two images side by side (but if just seeing them side by side is all you want, then you don't have to read any further). Compare view helps you narrow things down to find the best single photo out of a group of similar photos. It starts with the first two photos you selected: on the left is the Select image (it assumes this is the best image out of the bunch so far), and on the right is the Candidate (the photo hoping to beat the Select). Now, look at the two images. If the one on the right—the Candidate—is indeed a better photo than the one on the left, then you can go down to the toolbar beneath the Preview area and click the Make Select button (shown circled above). This moves that image on the right over to the left, making it the Select (the best photo), a new Candidate (the next image you'd selected) appears, and you compare the two again. If the Candidate isn't as good as the Select, then you'll just press the Right Arrow key (either in the toolbar or on your keyboard) to move the next Candidate into place. That's the process: If the Candidate looks better than the Select, you click the Make Select button and it becomes the image to beat. If not, you press the Right Arrow key. You'll keep doing this until you've run out of selected images, and then the image on the left at the very end is the best image in that group. It's like a tennis match using brackets. At the end, only one player (in this case, image) is left and that's the champ. When you're done, press **G** to return to Grid view.

How Do I... Find the Best Photo Out of Similar Photos?

Use Survey view. I think of this as the process-of-elimination view where, in the Library module's Grid view, you select a bunch of similar images (like these 12 you see above), and then you press the letter **N** on your keyboard. Then, what I do is look for the weakest photo in the bunch (believe me, it's easier to find the one you like the least than it is to find the one you like the most). Next, just move your cursor over the one you like the least (in this case, it's the second one in the second row) and a little black X appears in the bottom-right corner of the thumbnail. Click on it, and that image is removed from the screen (eliminated). It's not deleted from Lightroom or removed from your computer—it's in no danger whatsoever—it's just literally removed from the screen you're looking at to help you find the next image that is weak. Keep removing the weak images until all that's left are the best ones. Mark those as a Pick or a 5-star or whatever—whichever ones are still visible on-screen all get that rating. That's how I use Survey view to narrow things down to the best shots from a shoot, especially handy when you have a set of photos or poses that are very similar.

How Do I... Add More Photos to a Collection?

When you're working in the Library module and you see an image, either one you just imported or one in a different collection, and you want to add that image to an existing collection, just click on the image and drag it directly onto the collection you want it to go in (as seen above). You'll see the collection highlight and a little green circle with a + (plus sign) on it appear when you're right over the collection. Just release the mouse button to drop that photo into that collection.

ROB FOLDY AND SCOTT KELBY

Before you can start searching for people by name, you have to tell Lightroom who is who in your photos. You can do that manually, picture by picture, but Lightroom can help you by recognizing faces automatically, and then you just tell it whose face that is, and it will try to automatically find more instances of that particular person's face and tag it with their name (sometimes, it's actually right). To enter People (face-tagging) view, from the Library module, press the letter **O** or click on the little face icon in the toolbar below the thumbnail grid. This brings up the message above right, asking if you want to find as many faces as possible, or just those in the current collection. If you click Start Finding Faces in Entire Catalog, it's going to take a while, so for now, start by choosing Only Find Faces As-Needed and it starts bringing up faces in your current collection. It displays them in Grid view and up in the top-left corner of each thumbnail, it shows you how many faces it detected that are similar to that thumbnail. In the text field below a thumbnail, type in that person's name, and it tags all those shots with that person's name, and you're on your way. It takes a little time doing this the first time (going through all your faces and tagging who is who), but then you can search for anyone by name (in the Library Filter bar's Text search field—press the **\[backslash] key**, if you don't see it) or use the People tab in the Keyword List panel to display a list of people by name (just click on their name to see only that person).

If instead of just removing an image from a collection, you actually want the image out of Lightroom altogether (or off your computer and out of your life altogether), start in the Library module's Grid view and click on the image you want to delete. Now, go over to the left side Panels area and, in the Catalog panel, click on All Photographs, as seen above (otherwise, you'll just be removing the photo from a particular collection, and the image will still be in Lightroom, just no longer in a collection). Then, press the Delete (PC: Backspace) key on your keyboard and it will bring up the dialog you see above. It asks if you want to Delete from Disk (this moves the image out of Lightroom into the Trash [PC: Recycle Bin] for permanent deletion from your computer) or Remove (which leaves the actual image file alone—it's still on your computer—but removes the thumbnail and any traces of it from Lightroom, so you won't see it anymore).

To keep collections that are similar together (for example, let's say you went on vacation to Italy and you have collections for Vernazza, Portofino, Rome, Luca, and Sienna, so you have five different collections but they're tied together), we organize them by using collection sets. (A collection set is kind of like a main folder you put all the collections in to keep them together and make them easy to find.) So, in this case, you'd create a collection set called "Italy Trip" (or name it whatever you like, but France Trip or Egypt Trip would just be weird), and then drag those five collections into your Italy Trip collection set (as seen above), and they now appear all together, in alphabetical order, inside that set. Besides the organization, now anytime you want to see *all* of your images from your Italy trip, you just click on the Italy Trip collection set. Of course, to just see images from one city, simply click on its collection.

To stack a bunch of similar photos under one single thumbnail (helpful if you have multiple bracketed exposures for HDR, or for organizing the frames you want to merge together for a pano), in the Library module, select the images you want to stack (here, I've selected nine images of the same exact scene), then Right-click on any of those selected thumbnails and, from the menu that appears, under Stacking, choose **Group into Stack**, as shown above, on the left. Now those nine images all appear stacked under just one thumbnail image (see the little white box with a 9 in the upper-left corner above, on the right? That's letting you know that the thumbnail represents nine images). To expand the stack, click once on that little number (in this case, the number 9). To collapse the stack, just click on it again.

How Have Lightroom Automatically
Do I... Sort My Photos Using Auto-Stack?

In the Library module, go under the Photo menu, under Stacking, and all the way at the bottom, choose **Auto-Stack by Capture Time**, which brings up the dialog you see above. You can use the slider to choose the amount of time that passed between images to automatically have them stacked together under the same thumbnail. Click Stack, and you'll see all the stacks, with the number of images stacked under each thumbnail displayed in a white box in the upper-left corner of a thumbnail. To see the images in a stack, either click on its white box with the number, or click on its thumbnail and press the letter **S** on your keyboard. Here, I stacked images together that were taken 1-second apart or less. If you have images that you took in rapid succession, maybe you were doing bracketed shots for creating an HDR (or you just like shooting bracketed), or you shoot a lot of panos, this works really well for tidying up your collections.

Get Images from Lightroom on My Laptop to Lightroom on My Desktop?

In the Library module, go to the Collections panel and Right-click on the collection you want to move to another computer. In the pop-up menu that appears, choose **Export this Collection as a Catalog**, as shown above. This brings up a standard Save dialog, where you can name this catalog (I always name mine the same name as it appears in my Collections panel), but below the naming and saving part, make sure the Export Negative Files (so the actual photos will move along with the catalog) and Include Available Previews (so the thumbnails go along, as well) checkboxes are turned on. The center choice, Build/Include Smart Previews, is optional (I usually leave this off myself). Now, click Export Catalog and it saves the images, thumbnail pre-views, and the catalog file of just that one collection in one nice, tidy folder. Copy that entire folder onto an external hard drive, USB drive, etc., plug that drive into your other computer, and copy that folder onto your main computer (or onto your external drive, if that's where you store your photos). Then, go under Lightroom's File menu and choose **Import from Another Catalog**. Navigate to the catalog you just copied onto that computer, choose it, click Import, and that collection is added to Lightroom on your main computer with all the changes, edits, and organization you applied on your laptop still intact, as if you created it here in the first place. Once it's imported, you can delete the catalog you copied onto your new drive but do not delete the actual images, because...well...those are the real actual images.

In the Library module's left side Panels area, click on the little + (plus sign) button on the right side of the Collections panel's header, and choose **Create Smart Collection** to bring up the Create Smart Collection dialog you see above. This is where you choose the criteria for your smart (automated) collection from the pop-up menus. Click on the first option on the left and you'll see a long list of attributes you can choose from, and once you choose one, the next pop-up menu over is for modifiers (for example, if you choose Rating, your modifier might be Is Greater Than, Is Less Than, Is Equal To, and so on). If you need another modifier (like for Rating, where you need to choose the number of stars—1 through 5), that would appear next. To add another criterion, click the + button to the far right of this string of pop-up menus. To delete any criterion, click the – (minus sign; I didn't actually have to say that last one, did I?). When you're done picking criteria, click the Create button and Lightroom will pull all the images that fit that criteria into a new smart collection. By the way, you can change the criteria for your smart collection anytime by just double-clicking directly on it in the Collections panel (you'll know it's a smart collection because it will have a small gear icon before its name).

Edit Color Label Set

Preset: Lightroom Default (edited)

Delete	6
Not Edited	7
Final for Client	8
In the Running	9
Not Approved Yet	

If you wish to maintain compatibility with labels in Adobe Bridge, use the same names in both applications.

Cancel   Change

Go to the Library module, under the Metadata menu (up top), under Color Label Set, and choose **Edit**. This brings up the dialog you see above, where you can just type in the names you want, and even save them as a preset if you like by going under the Preset pop-up menu up top and choosing **Save Current Settings as New Preset**.

How Do I... Make a Collection a Target Collection?

In the Library module, if dragging-and-dropping images from your thumbnail grid into a particular collection starts to feel tedious, instead of all the dragging-and-dropping, you can make that collection a target collection by Right-clicking on it (over in the Collections panel, in the left side Panels area) and choosing **Set as Target Collection** from the pop-up menu (you can also make any collection the target collection when you first create it by turning on the Set as Target Collection checkbox in the Create Collection dialog). Now, when you see an image you like, just press the letter **B** on your keyboard, and it's added to your target collection instantly.

To delete all your rejected photos (photos you marked with the black flag by pressing the letter **X**), in the Library module, go under the Photo menu (up top) and choose **Delete Rejected Photos** (it's at the very bottom of the menu). This displays all your rejected photos and gives you one last look at them before they're gone. It also brings up a dialog asking if you just want them out of Lightroom (click the Remove button) or out of your life (click the Delete from Disk button).

When you have an image open in Loupe view **(E)**, to enter Lights Out mode, first press Shift-Tab to hide all the panels, then press the letter **L** on your keyboard two times, and you get the look above. This is different than full-screen mode in three ways: (1) Lights Out mode puts a thin white border around your image, (2) it's not a full-screen view—it fits within your Lightoom window, and (3) if you just press the letter L one time, instead of going to Lights Out mode (solid black), you go to Lights Dim mode, which leaves the interface visible, just darkening it, so you can still makes adjustments (though if you hit Shift-Tab first, it hides all the panels and stuff, so if you like Lights Dim mode, I'd skip hitting Shift-Tab altogether and just press L once and you're there). When you're done with Lights Out mode, just press L again to return to the normal view.

How Do I... Use a Quick Collection (and What Are They For)?

To add an image you have selected to your Quick Collection, just press the letter **B** and it's added (as long as you haven't set a different target collection, see page 42). To see the images in your Quick Collection, either go to the Catalog panel (in the Library module's left side Panels area) and click on Quick Collection, or choose **Quick Collection** from the pop-up menu at the top left of the Filmstrip along the bottom. The Quick Collection is just a temporary place to keep some images—maybe you just need a collection for an hour or so, and then you're done with it. This one's already set up with a keyboard shortcut to send images there, so it's helpful for sorting, or grabbing an image or two from different searches, or for anything where you know you'll have to delete the collection later, so why not just use a temporary collection? If, for some reason, you decide to turn the images inside your Quick Collection into a regular collection, then you can just Right-click on Quick Collection in the Catalog panel, and choose **Save Quick Collection**. This brings up a dialog where you can name your new collection (there's a checkbox there if you want to clear out the images from the Quick Collection once your new collection is saved). *Note:* If you have previously set a collection as the target collection, you'll need to Right-click on your Quick Collection and choose **Set as Target Collection**.

Photos with "AFC North" keyword

In the Library module, go to the Keyword List panel (in the right side Panels area) and it lists all the keywords you've assigned to photos. To the right of each, it shows you how many images have that particular keyword applied. If you want to see only the images that have a particular keyword assigned to them, move your cursor just to the right of the number and a little white arrow will appear. Click on that arrow (as I did here, where I clicked on the one next to the AFC North keyword), and now only the images tagged with that keyword are visible onscreen. You can also use the Library Filter bar at the top of the Preview area (if you don't see it, just press the \ [backslash] key on your keyboard). Click on the Text tab, choose **Keywords** from the first pop-up menu, then type in the keyword you're searching for, and only the images that have that keyword applied will appear. The downside to using this is that you have to know which keyword you're searching for, whereas the Keyword List will show you a list of all the words—when you see the one you want, you just click that right-facing arrow to the right of the number. By the way, the checkbox on the left shows which keywords have been assigned to a particular image, so you might have one image with five different keywords. Also, if you select some images and you see an asterisk beside one of those keywords in the list, it means that particular keyword isn't assigned to every one of those selected images— maybe just two or three.

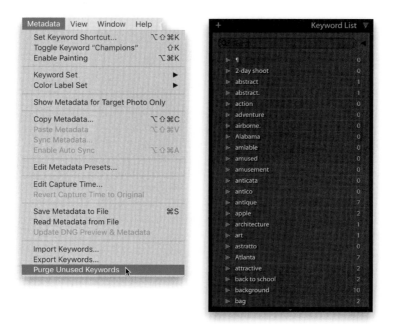

If you look in the Keyword List panel, in the Library module's right side Panel area, and notice that you have a bunch of keywords that have a zero (0) beside them, that means there are no images in your library that have that keyword assigned to them. To quickly clean up your keyword list (and get rid of all those keywords that you aren't using), just go under the Metadata menu and choose **Purge Unused Keywords** (as shown above).

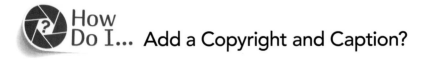

In the Library module, click on the image you want to embed copyright or caption info into, then go over to the Metadata panel (in the right side Panels area; make sure it is set to Default at the top), click in the Copyright field, and enter your copyright info (don't forget to change your Copyright Status to **Copyrighted** from the pop-up menu just below it). The Caption field is right above the Copyright field—just click in the caption field and start typing. If you're just adding a copyright, you can automate the process and apply the copyright to your images when you first import them into Lightroom—go check out page 4 in Chapter 1.

As long as your image has GPS location data embedded into the file, in the Library module, in the Metadata panel (in the right side Panels area), scroll down to GPS, and to the far right of that field you'll see an arrow. Click on that arrow and it will switch you to the Map module and display a map of the exact location where that photo was taken, as seen above.

If your images already have GPS data embedded into them, you don't have to do anything other than click on the Map module up top, and you'll see a red pin on the world map where those images were taken. If you click on the pin—boom—there are all your images from Greece (of course, this will only happen if you click on the pin that's located on Greece on the map. You knew that, right?). Anyway, it organizes your images on the map (it's just another way of getting to your images, and since it uses your already built-in GPS data, it's also a totally automated method). What if you don't have a GPS feature on your camera? Well, then you can add your images to the map manually. Just go up to the Search field at the top of the map and type in the location where you took the images. When you see the area where you took the shot(s), go down to the Filmstrip, select the images, drag-and-drop them on that spot, and it assigns that GPS location to your shots, adding a tag to the map, so now those images are one click away on the map.

How Do I... Create a New Lightroom Catalog?

Go under the File menu and choose **New Catalog**. This closes your current cat-alog and creates a completely new, completely empty catalog with no images, no thumbnails, no nuthin'. To return to your previous catalog, go under the File menu, under Open Recent and you'll find it in the list right there (of course, if you just created your first new catalog since you started using Lightroom, it's going to be a pretty short list).

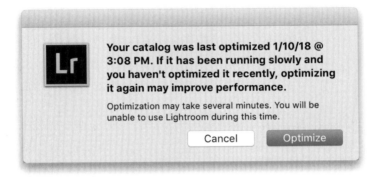

If Lightroom starts to feel a little sluggish, maybe it's time to optimize your Lightroom catalog (this can happen after using the same catalog for a long time, with lots and lots of photos in that one catalog). To do this, go under the File menu and choose **Optimize Catalog**. This brings up a dialog letting you know how long it has been since you last optimized it (you can see mine was *way* overdue). Just click Optimize and it does the rest (the bigger your catalog of images, the longer it will take, but it shouldn't take more than five minutes). When it's done, your catalog is optimized and you should be running...well...optimally.

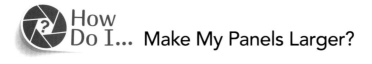

How Do I... Make My Panels Larger?

Just move your cursor right along the edge (the edge closest to your image[s], not the outside edge), as shown above, and your cursor will change into a two-headed arrow (shown circled here in red). Now, just click-and-drag to make your panels larger or smaller (your panels will only get so thin—they need a certain amount of space for the sliders and such to work—but they can get really wide if you want them to, just keep dragging in toward your image[s]).

How Do I... Create a Collection or a Collection Set from a Folder?

Go to the Folders panel and Right-click on the folder you want to create a collection from, and a pop-up menu appears. If this folder has other folders inside it, you can keep all that organization intact by choosing **Create Collection Set**. This will create a new collection set from that folder and all the folders inside it will appear as individual collections inside that set (collection sets are used for organizing collections). If it's just a folder full of images (with no subfolders inside), then instead, choose **Create Collection**.

To add a color label to a folder in the Folders panel, just Right-click on one and, from the pop-up menu that appears, under Add Color Label, choose the color you'd like (as seen above). The color label will appear to the far right of the folder's name in the Folders panel (in my Folders panel here, you'll see that I added a blue and a green color label to the two folders above the selected folder). To remove a color label, go under the same menu, but choose None. Just in case you were wondering if this same feature is available for collections, at this point, it's not. Weird, I know. Besides the visual advantage of tagging a folder with a color label, you can use the filtered Search option at the top of the Folders panel to search through just folders with color labels. To do that, click-and-hold on the magnifying glass icon, in the left of the Search field, and choose **Labeled Folders** to filter your search to only labeled folders (it hides everything but the labeled folders). Lastly, while we're here, right above Add Color Label in the pop-up menu is Mark Favorite. This marks your se-lected folder as a favorite (you'll see a little star icon at the bottom right of the folder icon), so not only can you now use the filtered search to narrow your search down to just the folders you marked as favorites, it also adds that folder(s) under Favorite Sources in the pop-up menu at the top left of the Filmstrip (see page 26).

How Do I... Move My Lightroom Photos to a Different Hard Drive?

Plug your new hard drive into your computer. When you look in Lightroom's Folders panel, it won't recognize this new hard drive because it only recognizes drives that have worked with Lightroom before. So, on the right side of the Folders panel's header, click on the + (plus sign) button and choose **Add Folder**. This brings up the Open dialog where you can access that new drive. Once you've chosen it, create a new folder on that hard drive, and now, since you created that folder from within Lightroom, it will recognize that external hard drive. You'll now see that external hard drive listed in the Folders panel and you can drag-and-drop folders directly onto it right in the Folders panel, and Lightroom won't lose track of your photos since you did all this moving within Lightroom.

Go under Lightroom's Help menu and choose **Updates**. When the Adobe Creative Cloud window appears, click on the Apps tab, and then scroll down until you see Lightroom Classic CC. If the button to its right says "Update," your version of Lightroom is not up to date, so click on it to update to the latest version of Lightroom Classic. If, instead, that button says "Open," your version of Lightroom is already up to date.

How Do I... Copy a Photo (or Photos) from One Collection to Another?

If you're looking inside a collection in Grid view and you want to copy one or more of these images into another collection, just select the images (click on the first image, then Command-click [PC: Ctrl-click] on any other images you want to copy), and simply drag-and-drop them into the other collection where you want them copied in the Collections panel. This leaves the images in their original collection and makes a copy of the thumbnails and places them in the collection where you dragged them.

How Do I... Back Up My Lightroom Catalog?

Back Up Catalog

Note: This only backs up the catalog file, not your photos.

Back up catalog: Once a week, when exiting Lightroom

Backup Folder: /Users/scottkelby1/Dropbox   [Choose...]

Also: ☑ Test integrity before backing up
☑ Optimize catalog after backing up

[Skip until next week]   [Skip this time]   [Back up]

When you quit Lightroom, a dialog will appear asking if you want to back up your catalog. Simply click the Back Up button and it makes a backup copy of your catalog and puts it in a folder named "Backups" in the same folder where your main catalog is stored. By the way, your catalog contains all your sorting and organization, all the edits you've made to your photos, all your Pick flags and star ratings, and well… everything you've done in Lightroom. So, having a backup copy (in case your catalog ever gets corrupted and you're unable to open it, which very rarely happens, or if your computer's hard drive crashes, or if your computer gets stolen or damaged) is important—you definitely want a backup, so you're not starting all over again from scratch with Lightroom. By default, it wants to save this backup to the computer you're running Lightroom on, but if your hard drive crashes or your computer gets stolen, you'll lose your backup copy, too. That's why I recommend saving your backup to a different hard drive, or ideally to a cloud backup (maybe Dropbox, or the Creative Cloud if you have the full CC account, or Apple's iCloud Drive if you're a Mac user). That way, if you have to recover from a backup, your backup won't be trapped on a crashed or stolen computer. You choose where to store your backups in the Backup Up Catalog dialog—just click the Choose button to choose a separate hard drive (or cloud service) to back up your catalog to.

Chapter 3

How to Customize Lightroom

How to Make It Work Like You Want It to Work

Every piece of software ships with "default" settings for all its controls and Lightroom is no different, but luckily for us, Lightroom is infinitely customizable so we can pretty much set things up the way we want them. However, it wasn't always this way, because at one point in Lightroom's history, Adobe's engineers carefully debated each and every setting throughout the application to make sure the default settings would only appeal to users with an IQ equal to that of lint. But, a long time ago, deep within Adobe's headquarters, there was this one rebel engineer named "Luke," and he heralded the idea that Lightroom should offer end users a way to customize Lightroom to suit each individual's needs. Well, as you might imagine, Luke wasn't very popular in the hallways at Adobe, but then one day, a German engineer named "Hans" approached him and stated that he agreed with Luke's customizing idea, and together they formed an alliance to restore justice to the end users. Well, Adobe's head of Engineering at the time, Mr. Murray Yavin, didn't agree with this Rebel Alliance, and this eventually resulted in many of the engineers warring over these very ideals, which led to what many Adobe insiders still call to this day, "The Battle of Yavin." Anyway, things got so bad that eventually the government got involved and pretty soon a local senator was called in, in hopes of uniting the engineers, but it wasn't until Luke and Hans teamed up with rogue engineering ace Wedge Antilles that these customization features were actually added to Lightroom. To recognize Wedge's contributions to the Alliance, the popular "Wedge" salad (named in his honor) was born and is still available at most popular casual dining restaurants. True story.

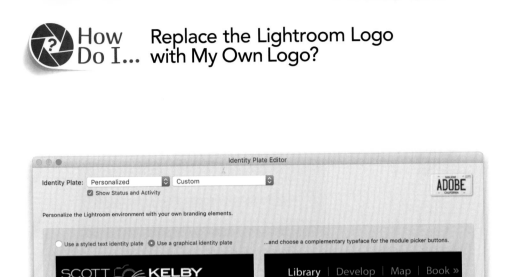

Go under the Lightroom (PC: Edit) menu and choose **Identity Plate Setup** to bring up the Identity Plate Editor (shown above). To replace the Lightroom logo with your own logo, choose Personalized from the Identity Plate pop-up menu at the top left of the dialog. Now, in the main section below, click on the Use a Graphical Identity Plate radio button, and then click on the Locate File button below the preview. Navigate your way to your logo, click Choose, and that's it—it replaces the Lightroom logo with your logo. If you don't have a logo graphic, you can change the Lightroom logo to your studio's name: just leave the Use a Styled Text Identity Plate radio button selected and type in whatever you'd like (the name of your studio, company, etc.). While your type is still highlighted, use the pop-up menus right below the text field to choose your font, font style (bold, italic, etc.), point size, and font color (click the little color swatch).

There's a ton of stuff you can have displayed (or choose not to have displayed) around your thumbnails in Grid view, and you choose what you want to see by pressing **Command-J (PC: Ctrl-J)**, which brings up the Library View Options. There are two main views: (1) Compact Cells, where the width of the cell stays the same but it's shorter because it displays less info. Another advantage is it has that nice big number in gray behind the image thumbnail (see the #30 above, bottom right), which I really like. (2) Expanded Cells is a taller cell to accommodate a lot more info, like badges and buttons, but you don't get the big image number (I totally don't get why this isn't an option. It's bigger, right? Why not let us have that big number? But I digress). Anyway, the best way to see what's available is to literally turn each checkbox on/off while looking at your cells. Also, if you choose Expanded Cells (shown, top right), you get four extra options near the bottom of the dialog: if you click on any of these pop-up menus, a huge list will appear and you'll be amazed at all the info you have to choose from (mostly, EXIF data that's embedded in the image), but since you have access to any four of these, you can pretty much put whatever you want around your thumbnail.

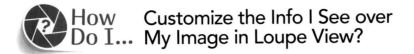

This info doesn't appear around the image, like the cell info. This info floats right over an image when you're in Loupe view (double-click on any image's thumbnail to enter Loupe view). Anyway, this is called the Info Overlay, and you can choose what info appears floating over your image. You do this in the same place you customize the cells, in the Library View Options dialog (press **Command-J [PC:Ctrl-J]**), but in the dialog, click on the Loupe View tab up at the top. There are two sets of info you get to customize, and you see them by pressing **Shift-I**—this toggles through Info 1, Info 2, and turns it off (so, if seeing this drives you crazy, now you know how to get rid of it). Choose what you want to see for each overlay from the pop-up menus in the Loupe Info 1 and Loupe Info 2 sections. There are a ton of options under those menus—just choose what you want to see displayed for each, then close the dialog, and you're all set.

You can turn on/off four different types of badges, which appear on and around your thumbnails down in the Filmstrip. Start by Right-clicking on any thumbnail to bring up a pop-up menu. Go to the bottom of that menu, under **View Options**, and you'll find these choices (seen above): Show Badges lets you see mini-versions of the same thumbnail badges you see in the standard Grid view (like the ones that show if a photo is in a collection, or whether keywords have been applied, or whether the photo has been cropped, or if it has been edited in Lightroom). Show Ratings and Picks will show you if your image has a star rating or Pick flag (you'll see little versions of those badges). If you choose Show Stack Counts, it shows how many images are inside a stack. Lastly, is Show Image Info Tooltips, which appear when you hover your cursor over one of your Filmstrip thumbnails—a little window will appear with the info that would normally display in Loupe view as Info Overlay 1. By the way, just like with regular Grid view badges, the tiny Filmstrip badges are "live" if you click on them (for example, if you click on a Crop badge, it takes you to the Crop Overlay tool in the Develop module), but you can always turn those off by going to this same menu and choosing Ignore Clicks on Badges.

How Do I... **Stop Scrolling through Panels So Much?**

To hide all the other panels, except for the panel you're working in right now, just Right-click on any panel header and choose **Solo Mode** from the pop-up menu. Now when you click on a panel, all the others collapse. Much faster and easier getting around (I absolutely love Solo mode!).

Just Right-click on any module's name up in the taskbar (as shown above), and a pop-up menu appears with a list of all the modules. By default, they're all checked because they're all visible. To hide any one you don't use (for example, I don't use the Map module), just click on it to deselect it, and now that module is hidden. Don't worry, if one day you want that hidden module back, you bring it back the same way, by Right-clicking and choosing it from the same pop-up menu.

How Do I... Temporarily Hide All the Panels?

It's one of my most-used shortcuts: **Shift-Tab** hides the top taskbar, the Filmstrip at the bottom, and the left and right side Panels areas, so your image can be viewed with minimum distractions (it does leave the toolbar along the bottom of the Preview area, though. If you want that hidden too, after you press Shift-Tab, just press the letter **T**). To bring everything back, press Shift-Tab again.

ADOBESTOCK/MAHOD84

Press the letter **F** to enter Full Screen Preview mode. Press it again to return to Normal mode. Thought it was going to be more complex than that, right? Usually, it is. ;-)

Look in the top-left corner of the Filmstrip and you'll see two buttons: one with a "1" and one with a "2" (seen above in the inset). Those are controls for your main and second displays. By default, "1" is always highlighted but if you have two displays connected, the "2" will be highlighted, as well—just click on it and a pop-up menu appears where you can choose what you want to appear on that second display (I generally choose the Loupe view myself). When you click on "1," its pop-up menu appears where you choose what you see on your main screen (I generally choose Grid view, as seen above. That way, when I click on a thumbnail in Grid view, it shows up huge on my second screen). The bottom section of the pop-up menus lets you choose how you want each screen to look—you can choose to see them full screen, or full screen but with the menu bar showing up top, and so on.

How Do I... Change the Color behind My Images?

Just Right-click anywhere on the background area behind your image and a pop-up menu appears with a list of different background color options.

How Do I... Stop the Side Panels from Popping In/Out?

Just Right-click directly on any of the little arrows at the center edges of Lightroom and a pop-up menu will appear. That "panel popping" is called "Auto Hide & Show" and to stop a panel area from poppin', just choose **Manual** from this pop-up menu (you have to do this for each panel area you want to stop poppin'). Now, to open or close a panel area, you'll click once on that same arrow at the edge of the panel area you want to open/close. Not Right-click; just click once to open/close. How to turn off this "Auto Hide & Show" is one of the most frequently asked questions I get.

Wait! I can make my font size bigger? You bet! Go to Lightroom's Preferences (under the Lightroom [PC: Edit] menu), click on the Interface tab, and in the Panels section up top, you'll see a Font Size pop-up menu. There are only two choices (and, no, I'm not going to list them here, but here's a hint: don't choose Small. Sorry, I couldn't help myself). Now, there is a catch: you have to restart Lightroom to actually see this new larger font size, but once you do, you'll dig it, especially if you're super old (I'm sorry. That was insensitive. Grandpa).

Chapter 4

How to Edit Your Images

Develop Module Stuff

This chapter is about editing your images, but at the end of the day (around 7:00 p.m.), I can only tell you which sliders do what—the actual act of editing your images is something that is very personal. Very private. Especially if you're editing naughty images, but you're not supposed to edit naughty images (they should always be just straight out of the camera), so we'll remove the private part, and just stick with personal. Now, when it comes to doing some serious image editing, I actually think it's very important that you create the proper editing environment and get in the "zone" and mindset of an artist. Some people think this means changing all the light bulbs in their studio to match a particular number on the Kelvin temperature scale or lowering the contrast and brightness on their display, so it looks like they're working on a monitor from 1998, but I think it's much more personal than that. First, start by setting the mood with some soft music. Instrumental songs work best, so your mind isn't distracted by the lyrics. I can't be trying to edit a beautiful landscape while the lyrics, "So, ladies! (Yeah!) Ladies! (Yeah!) If you wanna roll in my Mercedes. (Yeah!) Then turn around! Stick it out! Even white boys got to shout…" float through the airwaves—I need soft, calming cellos instead. I also recommend lowering the lights, and a glass of wine would be nice—perhaps a nice merlot like a 2010 Château Faizeau, Montagne-Saint-Émilion, from Bordeaux, France. Now, with everything in place, you may begin the art of editing. When you're done, and you see a beautifully edited image onscreen, then, and only then, is it acceptable to jump up and yell, "Baby got back!" *[LA face with an Oakland booty!]*

In the Develop module's Basic panel, drag the Exposure slider to the right to make your overall image brighter; drag it to the left to make it darker. There's more to setting your proper exposure than just this one slider, but this is the one I grab when I want my whole image a little brighter or darker. The Exposure slider doesn't cover the darkest areas (blacks) or the brightest (whites) in your image, but it covers the all-important midtone range (and then some). So, when it comes to exposure, it has the biggest overall effect on your image. In earlier versions of Lightroom, this slider was named "Brightness" because it controlled the overall brightness (although the math has been updated since it was Brightness, so while they were at it, they gave it the name "Exposure"). Anyway, knowing that old name helps give you some idea of what that slider does—it controls brightness.

That's the job of the Highlights slider in the Develop module's Basic panel—you simply drag it to the left to pull back those clipped highlights. Lightroom can tell you if your highlights are, indeed, clipping—just look at the triangle up in the top-right corner of the Histogram panel (at the top of the right side Panels area). That's Lightroom's highlight clipping warning, and if that triangle is white it means there's some serious highlight clipping in your image. To see exactly where that clipping is (and if where it's affecting matters to the image), click directly on the white trian- gle and any areas that are clipping will appear highlighted in red (as seen above in the Before image). Your goal is to drag the Highlights slider over to the left until that white triangle turns black (which means your clipping has been fixed). Also, if you see a red, yellow, or blue triangle (rather than white) that means there's some highlight clipping but only in that one color channel. So, the clipping isn't quite as serious as a solid white warning, which means there's clipping in all of your color channels, and you should probably deal with it.

If your photo looks kind of flat (especially compared to the image you saw on the back of your camera when you took it), one of the best quick fixes is simply to increase the contrast amount by dragging the Contrast slider (found in the Develop module's Basic panel) to the right. This does a number of things, besides just making the darkest areas of your image darker and the brightest areas brighter (which is pretty much what adding contrast does), because it makes the colors in your image appear much richer and more vibrant and our eyes perceive a more contrasty image as a sharper image, as well. Personally, I just use the Contrast slider, but if you feel you need more control, or more "juice," than just this one slider will provide, you can go to the Tone Curve panel. There, you can either use one of the Point Curve presets from the pop-up menu, or you can make the shape of any of those S-curve presets that have more contrast by clicking-and-dragging the points until the S-shape is steeper (the steeper the S-shape, the more contrast it creates). This Tone Curve contrast is stacked on top of anything you've already done with the Contrast slider, so you can go contrast crazy (once again, I rarely have to use this Tone Curve method because the Contrast slider by itself is actually very good. But, if you get in a contrast emergency, at least you know another place you can go to get help).

How Do I... Automatically Expand My Tonal Range?

In the Develop module's Basic panel, press-and-hold the Shift key and double-click directly on the word "Whites," or on its slider knob, and then Shift-double-click on the word "Blacks," or on its slider knob. This automatically expands the whites and blacks to their farthest points without clipping the highlights (well, that's the plan. Occasionally, the whites do create some minor highlight clipping), which expands your overall tonal range. If you've used Photoshop at all, you might re-member doing this same type of thing (although not automatically like this), but we used the Levels dialog to do it and it was called "setting your white and black points." This is the same thing; it's just automated (which is awesome). You might want to consider making this the first thing you do when you start to tweak an image, because you'll be starting with an expanded tonal range. Then, you can go back and tweak your Exposure amount (making the overall image brighter or darker) once the white and black points are set, but that Exposure adjustment will probably be very small, making the photo a little brighter or a little darker. This is how I set my exposure for every image: I Shift-double-click on Whites, Shift-double-click on Blacks, and then I move the Exposure slider a bit if I think I need my image to be a little brighter or darker overall. That's it.

Near the bottom of the Develop module's Basic panel, just drag the Clarity slider over to the right and the detail in your image gets immediately enhanced (what this is really doing is increasing the midtone contrast, so it makes your image look sharper even though it's really not sharpening). This Clarity slider is really great for bringing out any texture in your image, making metallic objects shiny, and making water look sparkling. However, keep an eye on the screen as you drag this slider because if you drag too far with it, you may start to get a black glow or halo around the edges of objects in your image, which is warning you that you're editing your image to death. How far you can drag this slider really just depends on the image— images like landscapes, cityscapes, automotive images, or anything with lots of very well-defined hard edges can take lots of Clarity. Other images, like portraits of people or flowers or things of a softer nature, can sometimes take very little because they'll start to look gritty.

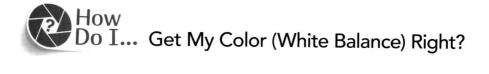

How Do I... Get My Color (White Balance) Right?

Get your white balance right and everything else falls into place. There are three ways to do this, and on this page, we'll tackle the automatic way, which is to: Try the white balance presets at the top of the Develop module's Basic panel. By default, the WB menu is set to As Shot, which means you're seeing the white balance as set in the camera when you took the shot. Click on that menu and a full list of white balance choices you could have chosen in-camera appears (the full list only appears if you shot in RAW. If you shot in JPEG, you'll only see As Shot, Auto, and Custom, and, by the way, Custom means "do it yourself by moving sliders," so it's not really a preset). Choose the preset that best matches the lighting when you took the shot. If you choose one that precisely matches the lighting situation (e.g., you shot in an office with fluorescent lights, so you choose Fluorescent) but it doesn't look good, just pick a different one. Who cares about the name? Choose the one that looks right to you. Also, if none of these are right on the money, then choose the one that's closest—that will be your starting place—then use the sliders that I talk about on page 83 to dial in just the right white balance.

How Do I... Set My White Balance Manually?

My favorite method for setting white balance is to use the White Balance Selector tool (the big eyedropper near the top of the Basic panel). All you do is click it on something light gray in your image. If there's nothing light gray, try to find something neutral (not too dark, not too bright, not too colorful). As you move your cursor around your image, you get a live preview of how the white balance adjustment would look for the area you're hovering over up in the Navigator panel at the top of the left side Panels area (as seen above). Very helpful.

If your goal is artistic and creative (rather than just "proper" white balance), then your tools will be the Temp and Tint sliders found near the top of the Basic panel. The nice thing about these sliders is that they're kind of self-explanatory. Want your image to look more blue? Drag the Temp slider toward blue. Want more magenta in your image? Drag the Tint slider toward magenta (like I did here). Between these two sliders, you can come up with tons of amazing colors for skies or for fashion looks or...well...whatever. I also somtimes use these sliders if I am trying to get an accurate white balance, but the White Balance presets didn't get me there. I choose the preset that looks the best, then I tweak the Temp and Tint sliders until it looks good to me (as I mentioned back on page 81). But, when I use these sliders, I'm usually trying to make the color in a landscape or travel shot look amazing, or I'm taking too much yellow out of someone's skin tone (by dragging toward blue), or I'm adding warmth to their skin (by dragging toward yellow).

Don't touch the Saturation slider—that will just make the colors in your image look "clowny." You just want "more colorful," which is why you want the Vibrance slider (found at the bottom of the Develop module's Basic panel) instead. It's kind of a "smart" Saturation slider because when you drag it to the right, it makes any dull colors more vivid. It hardly affects already vibrant colors (which is good) and it tries to avoid flesh tones altogether, so it doesn't make people in your photos look sunburned or jaundiced. It's also good for desaturating just a little bit if you have an overly colorful image—just drag it to the left a bit.

In the Develop module's HSL/Color panel (in the right side Panels area), click on "HSL" (Hue, Saturation, and Luminance), and then click on Saturation up top. To make any one of these colors more saturated (say you want all the reds in your photo to be more intense), drag its slider to the right (so, you'd drag the Reds slider to the right). To decrease the amount of any color, drag its slider to the left. If you're not sure which colors control which parts of your image, then use the TAT (the Targeted Adjustment Tool) found at the top left of the panel (the tiny target icon). Click on it, move it out over the area of color you want to adjust—like a blue sky or green grass—and click-and-drag it upward to increase that color's saturation (and any associated colors. For example, the sky might be made up of not just blues, but aquas, as well. It knows this, and will move both sliders automatically as you drag). Click-and-drag downward to reduce the amount of that color. To change the brightness of any one of the colors, click on Luminance, then click-and-drag the TAT downward on the area you want to adjust, and the color gets deeper and richer. (*Tip:* Drag the Blues to the left in the Luminance tab to make your skies a deeper blue and more epic.) If instead of enhancing color, you want to change a color (say you want to change someone's yellow shirt to green), click on Hue up top, and then click-and-drag the TAT up/down on that yellow shirt until you get the color you want. *Note:* This doesn't just change that one color in that one area—it changes all the similar colors in the image. So, if you have a blue sky, and your subject is wearing a blue shirt, know that both will change when you make an adjustment to one blue area.

To open up those shadows to be more like what our eyes saw when we took the photo, go to the Basic panel in the Develop module and click-and-drag the Shadows slider to the right. This backlit problem happens a lot because our eyes are so amazing that they can correct for a wide range of tones, tremendously more than even the most expensive camera sensor. So, while we're standing there in front of our subject, they don't look like a silhouette—we see them properly exposed. When we look through our DSLR camera's viewfinder, they still look properly exposed. But, when we press the shutter button and it passes the image to our sensor—which captures a much narrower tonal range—the result is your subject winds up looking like a silhouette. Luckily, that Shadows slider works wonders—just drag it to the right and watch the magic happen. *Note:* If you need to drag it way over to the right, one of these two things (may) happen: (1) Your image may start to look a little like an HDR image, in which case, try backing it off a bit; or (2) your image may lose contrast, in which case, just crank up the Contrast slider a bit. Again, this will probably only happen in certain images when you open the shadows way up.

How Do I... Crop to a Specific Size?

Click on the Crop Overlay tool (R), in the toolbar beneath the Histogram panel (in the Develop module's right side Panels area), and you'll see a bunch of tool options appear. There's an Aspect pop-up menu there and, by default, it's set to Original. Click on that pop-up menu and a list of preset sizes and ratios appears. Just click on the one you want and the cropping border instantly changes to reflect that aspect ratio.

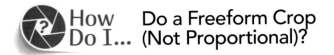

How Do I... Do a Freeform Crop (Not Proportional)?

Start by clicking on the Crop Overlay tool (its keyboard shortcut is the letter **R**) in the toolbar right below the Histogram panel (in the Develop module's right side Panels area). Then, in the tool options that appear, click on the gold lock icon (in the top right) to unlock the feature that keeps the current ratio in place and now you can drag each side individually, instead of it all moving at once (proportionally). Once you've unlocked the aspect ratio, you can also just grab the Crop Frame tool (in the top left; it looks like an angle ruler) and click-and-drag it out over your image in the shape you'd like (don't let it throw you that there's already a cropping border in place the moment you engage the Crop Overlay tool—just click-and-drag on your image like it wasn't even there and it will update immediately).

There are a number of ways to do this, so let's start with clicking on the Crop Overlay tool **(R)** right under the Histogram panel (in the Develop module's right side Panels area). In the tool options that appear right below, click the Auto button and it attempts to do an auto straighten. If there's something like a horizon line or a straight wall, it usually has no problem straightening out your photo with that one click. You can also click-and-drag the Angle slider, which rotates your image, and to help you make it straight, it puts a little grid of horizontal and vertical lines over your photo (it only appears while you're using this slider). If you think Lightroom needs a little help to know what's supposed to be straight, near the top left of the Crop Overlay options, there's a Straighten tool (it looks like a level). Click on it and then click-and-drag it along an edge in your image that is supposed to be straight (like that doorway in the back in the image above), and it straightens your photo. In a landscape photo, you'd drag it along the horizon line, or in a cityscape, along the sidewalk, or the side of a building (it doesn't have to be a horizontal line that's used to straighten). Lastly, you could just freestyle rotate the photo until it's straight: Click on the Crop Overlay tool and move your cursor just outside the cropping border, and your cursor will change into a two-headed arrow. Now, just click-and-drag in the direction you want to rotate, stop dragging when the image looks straight, and then press the **Return (PC: Enter) key** to lock in your crop.

To make a virtual copy (an image that looks like the original and acts like the original, but doesn't take up any space, so you can make as many virtual copies as you like and experiment to your heart's content), click on an image then press **Command-'** (apostrophe; **PC: Ctrl-'**). Your virtual copy appears right next to your original in the Develop module's Filmstrip and in the Library module's Grid view (that curled-page icon in the bottom-left corner of its thumbnail lets you know it's a virtual copy). Now, you can mess with this copy all you want. I use this for trying out different white balances on the same image. Here, I made eight virtual copies (one original and eight copies are shown above), so I could try a different white balance for each one, and then I displayed them all onscreen at the same time by selecting them all and pressing the letter **N** to enter Survey mode (which is what you're seeing above).

How Do I... Do Basic Sharpening?

Go to the Sharpening controls at the top of the Detail panel (in the Develop module's right side Panels area). The Amount slider controls the amount of sharpening (please forgive me for explaining that one). The Radius slider determines how many pixels out from an edge the sharpening will affect, and I usually leave this set at 1.0. If I run into an image that needs to be super-sharp, I'll occasionally move it up to 1.1, or even as high as 1.3, but that's it. The next slider down is Detail. I recommend leaving this set as-is (I'm not usually a fan of default settings, but this one is actually good). This slider, set where it is, allows you to apply a higher amount of sharpening without seeing halos around the edges of objects in your image (a typical side effect of too much sharpening), so it's an improvement on Photoshop's Unsharp Mask filter. If you want sharpening that looks more like Photoshop's (hey, ya never know), then raise this slider to 100 and it's pretty much the same (you can expect to see halos fast if you set the Amount slider too high). Last is the Masking slider. I only use this when I don't want the entire image sharpened equally—I just want the edges sharpened. For example, if I'm sharpening a woman's portrait, I want to sharpen her eyes, eyebrows, lips, edges of her face, etc., but avoid sharpening her skin because it brings out texture we don't want to enhance. By raising the Masking amount, it narrows the sharpening to just the edges. Press-and-hold the Option (PC: Alt) key as you drag the slider to see what it's affecting. Areas that turn black (as seen in the inset above) are not being sharpened—only the white areas get sharpened.

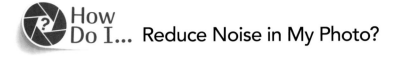

How Do I... Reduce Noise in My Photo?

Go to the Detail panel (in the Develop module's right side Panels area), and you'll see the Noise Reduction section right below Sharpening. There are two parts to this section: The Luminance slider reduces the noise specks you see in an image by slightly blurring the image (that's pretty much what noise reduction does—it hides the noise behind a blur). If you drag the Luminance slider to the right and you start to see that you're losing either detail or contrast in the image, you can use the two sliders right below to add them back. You'd use the Color slider if you saw red, green, and blue specks in your image—this does a good job of desaturating them, so you don't see them. Dragging this slider too far to the right can, once again, cause a loss of detail, so you can bring back some of that detail using the Detail slider below. The Smoothness slider is different—it doesn't bring back stuff. You'd use this to smooth out larger patches of color noise—just drag it to the right to help smooth those patchy areas out (you probably won't see these larger patches unless you're brightening up a really dark area in your image). Keep this one thing in mind when you're reducing noise: Using this feature blurs your image, from a little to a lot, depending on how far you drag the sliders. So, think of this as a balancing act—your job is to find that amount at which the noise is reduced without the image getting too soft.

How Do I... Remove That Bulging Look?

To fix that lens distortion that causes things like doorways and buildings to look bloated, like they're bulging outward toward the viewer, go to the Len Corrections panel (in the Develop module's right side Panels area), click on the Profile tab, and first try turning on the Enable Profile Corrections checkbox. That alone will sometimes fix the problem (make sure you see your lens make and model in the pop-up menus below the checkbox. If you don't, choose it from those menus—usually just choosing the brand will be enough for it to find the exact lens you used from its internal database). If the profile correction helped, but not quite as much as you'd like, in the Amount section below it is a Distortion slider that lets you fine-tune the amount—just drag it to the right. If that still isn't enough of a fix, click on the Manual tab (as seen above), and then drag the Distortion Amount slider at the top to the right until the bulging flattens out (this will leave white gaps around your image, so you'll have to crop the edges away, or let Lightroom do it for you by turning on the Constrain Crop checkbox in the middle of the panel). Take a look at the Before image above; in particular, look at the center panel of the door on the left. It's bowing outward. Look at the windows, too—they're bowing outward to the sides, as well. Now compare it with the After image on the right and you'll see how nice and straight it looks now. That's what the Distortion slider does—it removes that bowing and lens distortion.

How Do I... Stop Buildings from Leaning?

To get rid of this keystoning effect (where buildings don't look upright—they're either leaning in, like in the Before image here, or leaning back, like they're going to fall over), first go to the Lens Corrections panel (in the Develop module's right side Panels area), and in the Profile tab, turn on the Enable Profile Corrections checkbox. This applies a built-in lens profile from Lightroom's database (this won't fix the problem, but it makes the thing that does fix it, which we'll do next, do a better job). If for some reason it doesn't find your lens, choose it from the Lens Profile pop-up menus, and that will usually be enough for it to find a profile (if not, choose it manually from the pop-up menu). Now go to the next panel down—the Transform panel—and in the Upright section up top, click the Auto button (as seen here). That will usually do the trick, though this often leaves white gaps in either (or both) of the sides, top, and bottom of your image. If that's the case, turn on the Constrain Crop checkbox at the bottom of the panel to have it automatically crop those white gaps away. If the Auto button doesn't do the trick, you can try Vertical or Full, or even Guided Upright (where you drag out two horizontal lines over things in your image that should be level, like a wall or the top of a building, and then you drag two vertical lines out, as well. This is for images that Auto, Vertical, and Full don't work for). Your final option is to do the correction manually using a slider: go down to the Transform section and drag the Vertical slider to the right until the building(s) looks straight (it stops looking like it's leaning in).

To get rid of edge vignetting (a problem caused by your lens), go to the Lens Corrections panel (in the Develop module's right side Panels area), and in the Profile tab, turn on the Enable Profile Corrections checkbox (your lens make and model should appear in the pop-up menus below. If it doesn't, just choose it yourself). That will often fix the problem right there, but if it doesn't quite do the trick, there's a Vignetting slider in the Amount section that lets you fine-tune the amount, so try that and see if it helps. If that still doesn't do the trick, then you'll have to do it manually: Click on the Manual tab and, near the bottom, you'll see two Vignetting sliders. Drag the Amount slider to the right to brighten the corners of your image, removing the vignetting problem. The next slider, Midpoint, controls how far your edge brightening extends into your image. If it's just right up in the corners, then drag the slider way over to the right. If it's a bit farther out, you might have to drag it to the left (basically, just drag the Midpoint slider back and forth a few times and you'll see what I mean).

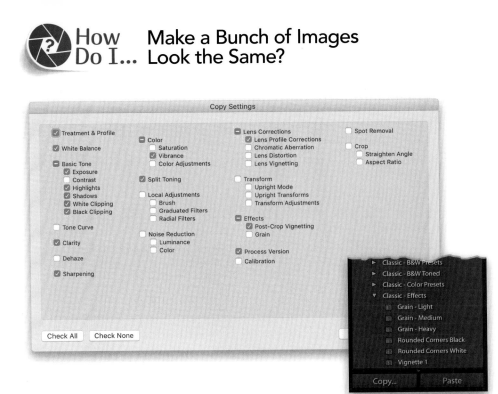

To copy the settings from one image and paste those same settings onto a bunch of other images (maybe they were taken in the same lighting conditions or they're shots that look very similar), click on the Copy button at the bottom of the Develop module's left side Panels area. This brings up a dialog asking which settings you want to copy. I usually click on the Check None button at the bottom, so it turns off all the checkboxes, then I just turn on those whose sliders I moved while making the edits to my currently selected photo, and then click the Copy button (by the way, make sure you always leave the Process Version checkbox turned on, so Lightroom continues to use the latest math. Turning this off turns on the old, outdated math, so we always leave this on). Now, go down to the Filmstrip, Command-click (PC: Ctrl-click) to select each photo you want to have these exact same settings applied to, then click on the Paste button (also at the bottom of the left side Panels area, right next to the Copy button). Those settings you copied are now applied to all those selected images at once.

First, down in the Filmstrip, select a bunch of images you want to edit (you have to select them first. This is important because if you don't select them first, the button you're going to need will be hidden). Then, at the bottom of the Develop module's right side Panels area, you'll see the Sync... button with a little switch to its left. Click on that switch and it turns on Auto Sync (one of my favorite of all Lightroom features). Now, while those images are all still selected in the Filmstrip, click on the image you want to work on and start making your edits. Any changes you make to this image (which Adobe calls "the most-selected image") will be immediately applied to all your other selected images at the same time. It's pretty much a "change one, it changes them all" type of edit, but it's one of those things that can save a load of time, especially when changing things like exposure or white balance across a lot of images.

How Do I... Undo My Changes?

To undo your last step, you can use the regular ol' Undo keyboard shortcut, **Command-Z (PC: Ctrl-Z)**. If you press it again, it undoes another previous step, and then another, and so on, until it gets back to how the original image looked when you imported it. If you want to see all the edits and changes you've made to the image since you imported it, go to the Develop module's History panel (in the left side Panels area), and there, you'll see each edit listed in order (with the most recent at the top). You can click on any one to jump to how your image looked at that stage of your edit, and you can always return your image to how it looked when you first imported it by scrolling to the bottom of the History panel and clicking on the entry called "Import." By the way, if you undo a step using the Command-Z keyboard shortcut, and then decide you want to "redo" that step, just add the Shift key to that Undo shortcut (so the Redo shortcut would be **Command-Shift- Z [PC: Ctrl-Shift-Z]**).

Start in the Develop module, near the top of the Basic panel, by choosing a RAW profile for your RAW photo (by the way, if you shoot in JPEG, you can skip this page). This lets you choose different methods for how Lightroom will interpret your RAW photo (basically, you get to choose the starting place for how your image will look before you start actually tweaking it with sliders and such). Today, the default RAW profile, Adobe Color, is actually pretty decent (much better than what we had for the past 11 years), and it's a pretty good all-around starting place for most images. However, if your image is a landscape or a nature or travel shot, you might want the colors to be more vivid and the image to be a bit more contrasty—more like the image you saw on the back of your camera when you took the shot (rather than the flatter-looking actual RAW image). So, you might try a different RAW profile, like Adobe Landscape or Adobe Vivid. Just choose one of those from the Profile pop-up menu and see how they look on your image. If you like one of these better, then go with that as your RAW starting place. If you're shooting portraits, try Adobe Portrait and see if you like that look better (there is no right or wrong answer here—choose whichever profile looks best to you. This is all personal preference). Keep in mind that one of the main things we use these profiles for is to make our flat-looking RAW image look more like the contrasty, vivid-looking JPEG preview that we saw on the back of our cameras, so you're starting in a better place. That way, you'll have less editing to do in the Develop module to get your image looking good.

If you want to reset any slider to its default, just double-click directly on the slider's knob. To reset an entire section of sliders, like all the sliders in the Tone section of the Basic panel, just double-click directly on the section's heading and it resets all those sliders to zero. This goes for the other sections in the Basic panel, too (they're circled in red above on the right), like Presence and even the WB (white balance) sliders, as well as sections in other panels.

To get rid of those green or purple lines along the edges of things in your image (like along a wall, or a building, where it almost looks like you traced along the edge with a thin magic marker), just go to the Lens Corrections panel, click on the Profile tab, and turn on the Remove Chromatic Aberration checkbox (that's the technical name for what you're experiencing—it's a lens issue, nothing you did wrong), as shown above on the left. Sometimes, just turning on that checkbox alone will do the trick, but if it doesn't, then click on the Manual tab, and in the Defringe section, drag the Amount sliders to the right a bit until the green or purple edge fringe goes away, as seen above on the right (look at the green and purple fringe along the edges of this castle, here. I zoomed way in so you could see it clearly). If you increase an Amount slider a bit (you usually don't have to drag it very far) and it's not affecting the color, you might need to expand the range of purples or greens it affects using the Purple Hue or Green Hue slider. To add more colors that it affects, drag the slider knobs farther apart—you may even have to drag the two Hue slider knobs to the right or left until it finds the right colors to neutralize. This feature works amazingly well and it just takes a few seconds, so if you see a chromatic aberration problem, it's worth the 10 seconds it takes to fix it.

Go to the Basic panel (in the Develop module's right side Panels area), and to the right of the word "Tone," click on the Auto button (as shown above), and Lightroom will take a stab at correcting your image for you. This Auto button was recently reworked by Adobe and it does a far better job than in previous versions (it uses machine learning and artificial intelligence to apply an auto image fix). However, it has been my experience that while it's better than it has ever been (by a long shot), it generally opens up the shadows too much and lowers the Contrast amount too much. So, when I use this feature, after I click it, I then drag the Shadows slider back a bit to the left, and then I drag the Contrast slider a bit to the right (how much depends on the particular image—you have to make a judgment call on what looks good to you). If you do those two things, it does a pretty decent job, and at the very least gives you a decent starting place to continue tweaking your image. By the way, if you don't like the results of the Auto button at all, you can always use Undo **(Command-Z [PC: Ctrl-Z])** to undo that auto correct and set you right back where you were, so there's no harm in giving it a click.

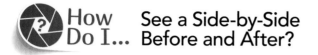

How Do I... See a Side-by-Side Before and After?

When you're in the Develop module, to see a side-by-side before-and-after view, just press the letter **Y** on your keyboard and—voilà—a side-by-side before/after appears onscreen. If you want to zoom in, press **Command–+ (PC: Ctrl–+)** and you get the tighter view you see above. If you press the letter Y again, you return to normal view (the after view). If you want to toggle through the different comparison views (left/right, top/bottom, and single-image split-screens of each), click the button with YY on it in the left of the toolbar, just to the left of the words "Before & After." To leave this mode altogether, press the rectangular button to the left of the YY button (or just press the letter **D**).

If you're in the Library module, go under the Photo menu, choose **Open in Reference View**, and it takes you over to the Develop module's Reference view. If you're already working in the Develop module, go under the View menu and choose **Open in Reference View** (or, in either module, you can just press **Shift-R**. If you had an image selected, just press **Command-D [PC: Ctrl-D]** to deselect it). Now, go down to the Filmstrip and click-and-drag the image you want to reference up to the Reference side (the left side) of the Preview area (this is the image you're trying to match—it may be an image from years ago, and it's now a JPEG, so you don't know what the original post-processing settings were, or maybe it's one you downloaded from the web and you're trying to match its look in Lightroom). Next, click on the photo in the Filmstrip that you want to edit to look like your Reference photo, so it appears as the Active image, and then use the panels on the right to do your editing. When you're done, press the letter **D** on your keyboard to return your edited image to regular Loupe view.

Near the top right of the Develop module's Basic panel, click on the little icon with four squares (to the right of the Profile pop-up menu) to open the Profile Browser. When you see a RAW or creative profile you want added to your Profile pop-up menu, move your cursor over it and click on the grayed-out star icon in the top-right corner of the profile thumbnail (as shown circled above right). Now that profile will appear in your Profile pop-up menu, as well as in the Favorites section near the top of the Profile Browser. To remove a profile from your Favorites, just click the star again to turn it "off."

How Do I... Hide Profiles I Don't Use?

Open the Profile Browser (near the top right of the Develop module's Basic panel, click on the little icon with four squares), then scroll down and Right-click on one of the profile set names. From the pop-up menu that appears, choose **Manage Profiles** (as shown above left) to bring up the Manage Profiles dialog (shown above right). Turn off the checkbox beside any of the profile sets you want to hide, then click the Save button. To bring them back, just go back to the Manage Profiles dialog and turn them back on. To quickly make them all visible again, just choose **Reset Hidden Profiles** from that same pop-up menu (seen just below Manage Profiles above left).

If you have a hazy or foggy image (like the one you see above on the left), go to the bottom of the Basic panel, to the Presence section, and drag the Dehaze slider to the right and it cuts through the haze like a knife cuts through I Can't Believe It's Not Butter®. There are three side effects of Dehaze, though, that I want to tell you about, so you can counteract them: (1) If you apply a heavy amount of Dehaze and there is any, even subtle, edge vignetting (darkening of the edges caused by the lens), it really exacerbates it (that's a 22-point word, by the way. "Exacerbates." Not "it"). So, if you see this start to happen when you apply a lot of Dehaze, reset the slider to zero, then go remove any edge vignetting (see page 95), and then go back and apply Dehaze. (2) If you apply a lot of Dehaze, it tends to boost the amount of blue in your image a lot (look at how blue it made the sky here, which in this case was a happy accident). If that's the case, go to the HSL/Color panel, click on the Saturation tab, and lower the amount of the blues by dragging the Blue slider to the left until the extra blue is gone. (3) Another way to avoid the boosted blues and edge vignetting is to use the Adjustment Brush (K) instead and just paint Dehaze where you need it, avoiding the sky and corners of your image. The Dehaze amount for the brush seems higher than the same amount in the Basic panel, so keep that in mind.

If you made adjustments to an image and you want to apply those exact same edits to another photo (without going through the whole copy-and-paste thing, with a dialog popping up asking which edits you want to copy-and-paste, like you learned on page 96), while you're in the Develop module do this: First, down in the Film-strip, click on the photo that has the edits you like, then scroll over to the image that you want to have the exact same edits. Click on it, then click the Previous button at the bottom of the right side Panels area (as seen above).

How Do I... Automatically Match Exposure Across Multiple Photos?

In the Library module, first select all the photos you want to have the same exposure. Now, click on the photo in that selected group that has the exposure you want them all to have (the highlight around this thumbnail will be brighter than the rest of the selected images. Adobe calls this the "most-selected image"), then switch to the Develop module. Go under the Settings menu up top, choose **Match Total Exposure**s (as seen above), and the other selected images will change their exposure to match the selected image's overall exposure as much as possible.

Chapter 5

How to Use the Brushes

The Adjustment Brush, the Spot Removal Brush, and All That Stuff

Not many people know this, but Lightroom's Spot Removal tool was originally created by an animator at The Walt Disney Studios during the production of the original animated feature *101 Dalmatians*, where it was used extensively for that scene where the dogs' spots fell off. They initially were going to have animators remove the spots from each dog by hand, rotoscoping each cell individually, but at 24 frames per second that would take an incredibly long time, which normally wouldn't be a problem, except that the IMAX 3D version of the movie was slated to open two weeks prior to the Hollywood theatrical release, and the Blu-ray version was set to release after just 5½ weeks in theaters, so their deadline was unmovable. Plus, Betty Lou Gerson (who voiced the part of Cruella De Vil) had already contracted with Republic Pictures to be in *The Red Menace* (in the role of Greta Bloch) whose filming was to take place in just nine days, so they needed a solution that would get the spots removed as quickly as possible without delaying the release. So, long story short, the studio called Adobe, told them they were using Lightroom extensively, and sent one of their top animators over to see if there was anything they could do to help the studio out of this jam. Well, as it turns out, an engineer there had been working on a tool for removing specks and dust from digital CMOS sensors, so Adobe rushed the release of Lightroom 4 to include the tool and, well, the rest is movie-making history. This story would have been all the more fascinating if it had been true, but of course it can't be because the original *101 Dalmatians* was released in 1961, about 46 years before Lightroom was even invented, not to mention the whole IMAX 3D, and Blu-ray, and all that technology I tossed in there just to getcha off track. I really gotcha with that whole "rotoscoping" line though, didn't I? Reeled ya right in. Come on, I kinda had ya going there for a minute. Or was it 5½ weeks?

In the Develop module, click on the Adjustment Brush (**K**) in the toolbar below the histogram in the right side Panels area. Near the top left of the Adjustment Brush panel, double-click directly on the word "Effect" to reset all the sliders to zero. To set the brush so that when you paint over an area it brightens it, drag the Exposure slider to the right and then paint. Once you paint over an area, you can go back to the Exposure slider and tweak the amount until it looks just right to you. If, instead, you want to darken as you paint, drag the Exposure slider to the left. Think of this as "painting with light." Also, you can do more than just brighten/darken (this was called dodging and burning back in the film darkroom days); you can add adjustments with any of the other sliders for those areas you painted over, as well.

It's an easy-to-remember shortcut: to hide the Edit Pins (seen circled above in red) on your image in the Develop module, just press the letter **H** on your keyboard. To bring them back, just press H again. If you just want them hidden temporarily, press-and-hold H and they'll stay hidden as long as you hold that key down. When you release the key, you can see the pins again.

To reset them to zero, just double-click directly on the word "Effect" near the top-left corner of the Adjustment Brush panel (in the Develop module's right side Panels area; as shown here circled in red), and it resets all the sliders to 0 (as seen above right). If you want the Adjustment Brush to have default settings, so each time you choose it, it starts with the same settings, here's how to do that: when you choose the Adjustment Brush **(K)**, before you click it anywhere within your image, drag the sliders to where you want them to be as your defaults. That's it—you just set the defaults. Each time you click New, at the top right of the panel, these same settings will appear.

In the Develop module, click on the Spot Removal tool (Q) in the toolbar near the top of the right side Panels area. Resize your brush, so it's a little bit larger than the speck or spot you want to remove (as seen above left), and just click once. The tool will sample a nearby area to use as a source for the removal (see the thicker second circle on the right above? That's where it's sampling from). If for any reason the fix looks odd (it picked a bad spot to sample from, which definitely happens from time to time), you can just click-and-drag that second circle—the one it's sampling from—to a different location to get better results. Also, you can click-and-drag on the edge of the circle to resize it, and you can click-and-drag the first circle (the one where you clicked—it has a thinner border) if you were a little off when you first clicked over the spot you want to fix. If you don't like the way the repair looks, you can have Lightroom automatically choose a different area to sample from, so you get a different result from the repair—simply press the / (Forward Slash) key on your keyboard and it picks a new spot. Just keep hitting that key until your repair looks good.

Get the Graduated Filter tool (**M**; it uses the same sliders as the Adjustment Brush, but it's not actually a brush—you click-and-drag it in a direction, like a gradient). Start by resetting all the sliders to zero (double-click on the word "Effect," as you just learned a couple of pages ago), and then drag your Exposure quite a bit over to the left. Now, take the tool and click-and-drag from the top of the image down to the horizon line, and it darkens the top, then gradually fades down to transparent, like a real neutral density gradient filter would if you put one on your lens. Of course, you can do more than just darken the sky: One of my favorite tricks is to drag the Temp slider over toward blue to make the sky much bluer. You can also boost the contrast (drag the Contrast slider to the right), or the vibrancy of the color in that part of the sky (drag the Saturation slider over to the right), and increase (or decrease) the highlights in the sky using the Highlights slider (I didn't end up doing that here), as well as adjust the Whites and Blacks.

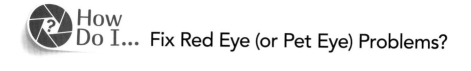

How Do I... Fix Red Eye (or Pet Eye) Problems?

Get the Red Eye Correction tool from the toolbar, near the top of the right side Panels area (right under the histogram), click the tool in the center of your subject's eye, and drag outward until it matches the size of the entire eye (not just the pupil and iris area, the whole eye). Lightroom will detect the pupil within that area, but if it doesn't fully remove the red, try dragging the Pupil Size slider in the tool's panel to the right. If it now looks too gray, just drag the Darken slider to the left. It works the same way with Pet Eye, but the results are tuned to the reflection from pets' eyes—just click the Pet Eye tab once you have the Red Eye Correction tool selected.

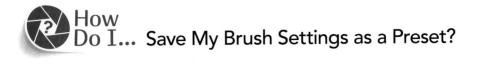

How Do I... Save My Brush Settings as a Preset?

In the Adjustment Brush panel, click on the word "Custom" just to the right of the word "Effect" and, from the pop-up menu that appears, right near the bottom of the menu, choose **Save Current Settings as New Preset**, as shown here. Give your new preset a name (seen above right), and now your preset will be added to this menu so you can get to those same brush settings in the future with just one click.

Click on the Adjustment Brush (**K**) in the toolbar near the top of the Develop module's right side Panels area, and near the top of the panel, immediately to the right of the word "Effect," you'll see the word "Custom." Click on it and a pop-up menu appears with a host of presets put there by Adobe with ideal settings for particular tasks. Choose **Soften Skin** from this menu (as shown here), and it puts in some pretty decent settings for skin softening. Now, all you have to do is take that brush and paint over your subject's skin to soften it (while remembering to avoid detail areas, like their eyes, lips, edges of their nostrils, eyelashes, eyebrows, and hair). Just for the record: I think the skin smoothing looks a bit too much here, but you can reduce the amount by using the tip on page 126.

If you make a mistake while painting with the Adjustment Brush, just press-and-hold the **Option (PC: Alt) key** and paint over the area where you messed up. When you do this (holding that key down), you're actually switching over to a different brush that's set up to erase the mask, and since this is a different brush, it actually has its own separate settings. These settings are found at the bottom of the Adjustment Brush panel, but you can't access them until you actually make a brush stroke (I know, it's weird). Once you paint a stroke, you can then click on the word "Erase" down at the bottom of the panel and set your settings for the Erase brush. Again, these Erase settings are only available after you've painted a stroke, then you can access them by either: (a) pressing-and-holding the Option key and they toggle as long as you hold that key down, or (b) you can just click the Erase button (as seen above left). *Note:* You can also erase parts of your Graduated Filter (in case there's an area you don't want to be affected by the filter), but it's different than the Adjustment Brush. Instead, click-and-drag your gradient, and you'll see a Brush button at the top right of its panel (as seen above right). Just click on it and then, once again, press-and-hold the Option key and erase over the areas you don't want affected.

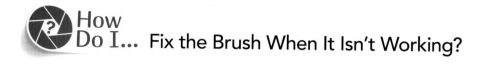

Brush : **A** **B**   Erase ▼

Size		14.5
Feather		0
Flow		9
☐ Auto Mask		
Density		13

Range Mask : Off

If you go to your Adjustment Brush and either it doesn't seem to be working right, or it seems very weak, there's a good chance that your Flow and/or Density settings are set very low, or are set to zero. Drag 'em back up and you should be up and running again. If your brush seems to be "skipping" or leaving gaps while you're painting, turn off the Auto Mask checkbox for smoother performance and much better coverage.

In the Develop module, when you're using the Spot Removal tool (Q) to remove distracting things near the edge of objects using the default Heal setting (which is where you want to keep it most of the time), it tends to smear (as seen above left on the edge of the wall). That's your cue to switch to the Clone setting (as seen in the inset and used on the edge of the wall above right). This just changes the method of removal and it usually fixes the smearing problem. Also, you might need to drag the Feather slider for the tool to the left and right and see which setting looks best for the current area you're working on—just a simple drag to the left and back to the right, and you'll find the sweet spot where it looks best.

To draw a straight line with the Adjustment Brush, click once with the brush, press-and-hold the Shift key, then move your cursor to where you want the straight line to end and click one more time, and it draws a straight line between the two points. Okay, how do you pull off the trick shown here where the brush goes from a small size at the top of the column to a much wider size at the bottom? You just click up top with a small brush size, then move your cursor down to the bottom of the column, but before you Shift-click, make your brush size the size of the bottom of the column, then Shift-click. It will automatically transition the size of the brush smoothly as it moves from the smaller size where you first clicked up top to the larger size at the bottom.

Turn on the Auto Mask checkbox (near the bottom of the Adjustment Brush panel)—this helps to keep you from accidentally having your brush spill over onto areas you didn't want affected by it. With this turned on, only the area under the little plus-sign crosshair in the center of the brush will be affected (see the image above where I'm painting on the wall on the bottom-left side of the staircase—I left the red mask overlay turned on [see the next page for more on this], so you could clearly see where I'm painting—and even though the edges of my brush are clearly extending over the wall, it doesn't brighten that area at all because the crosshair is still over the wall in the red mask tint). *Note:* Having this feature on does tend to slow the brush down a bit because it's doing a lot of math while you paint, trying to detect edges as it goes. Also, if you paint over an area and it seems to not cover the area evenly, you might turn off Auto Mask and repaint over that area. As a general rule, I leave Auto Mask turned off most of the time while I'm painting, but as soon as I get near an edge I don't want to affect, I turn it on for just that part of the edit.

When painting with the Adjustment Brush, you can either press the letter **O** or you can turn on the Show Selected Mask Overlay checkbox found down in the toolbar below the center Preview area. Turning this feature on can be really handy to be able to see the exact area you're affecting and specifically to see if you missed any areas (that's what I did here, where I saw that I missed an area between her hand on the left and her hair—that blue background area that isn't tinted in red. Now I know that's an area I need to paint over to add to my mask).

First, click the little down-facing black triangle near the top-right corner of the Adjustment Brush panel (shown circled here in red, above left). This collapses all the normal sliders down to just one Amount slider (seen above middle), and that slider controls the overall amount of all the sliders at once. Here, I dragged it over to the left, lowering the Amount of my changes, and then when I click on that triangle again to expand the panel and show all the sliders again, take a look (above right) at how much lower all the slider amounts are now, compared to what they were originally (above left).

How Do I... Duplicate an Edit Pin?

In the Develop-module's center Preview area, right-click on the pin you want to duplicate and, from the pop-up menu that appears, choose **Duplicate** (as seen here). This duplicate will appear directly on top of the original, so it'll look like nothing happened, but if you click-and-drag right on the edit pin you duplicated, you'll see you're dragging off a copy. Another way to do this is to press-and-hold Command-Option (PC: Ctrl-Alt), click on the pin, and drag it wherever you want it.

Build Up As I Paint (Like an Airbrush) When Using the Adjustment Brush?

Go to the bottom of the Adjustment Brush panel and lower the Flow amount to 25. Then, for example, if you wanted to increase the brightness as you paint, you'll drag the Exposure slider all the over to the right to 4.00 (to full power). Now, when you make a brush stroke, it will be a very slight amount of Exposure (see the white stroke on the far left above). If you paint another stroke over that area it will start to build up (as seen in the center stroke that's much brighter), and if you keep painting over that same area, it will build up and build up, like you see in the stroke on the far right. This gives you a level of control as you paint, rather than the other method of picking a random amount of Exposure, painting a stroke, then going back and dialing in the right amount using the Exposure slider again. This way, you paint and if the effect isn't enough, you just keep painting over the same area, slowly building up, until it looks just right to you.

Look at the images above. On the left is the original with its washed-out sky, and the center image has a Graduated Filter applied over the sky with the Exposure lowered 1 ½ stops and the Temp slider moved to the left to make it more blue. Here's the problem: that darkening also darkened the dome when all you want to darken is the sky. Now look at the far-right image. That area over the dome is perfectly masked away, and Lightroom can do this automatically. Here's how: After adding a Graduated Filter, go to the Range Mask section at the bottom of the Graduated Filter panel and from the Range Mask pop-up menu, choose **Color**. Now click on the eyedropper to the left of Range Mask, and then click it once on the color you want to mask away from foreground objects. Here, I clicked in the blue area to the right of the dome, and it masked that color away, so it doesn't affect the dome. If clicking once doesn't do the trick, you can mask additional colors by either Shift-clicking to add up to four more eyedroppers, or you can click-and-drag the eyedropper over a range of colors in an area to mask away. There's a second Range Mask feature: choose **Luminance** from the pop-up menu and then use the two sliders to mask based on the brightness/darkness of the object that's being affected (drag the sliders over once or twice, and you'll see how it works). Also, if you press-and-hold the Option (PC: Alt) key, it will display the mask it's creating for you (which helps in understanding what Range Mask is actually doing). One last thing: you also could have manually painted away the effect over the dome by choosing the Brush option in the Graduated Filter panel, pressing-and-holding the Option (PC: Alt) key, and carefully painting over the dome.

You're going to heavily blur a large area at the top of your image, and a large area near the bottom, leaving a thin area unaffected over one part of your image (as if you're peeking though a large slit in the blurriness, which is what creates the effect). Get the Graduated Filter tool **(M)**, from the toolbar beneath the Develop module's Histogram panel, and double-click directly on the word "Effect" near the top left of the panel to reset all the sliders to zero. Set the Clarity to –100 and the Sharpness to –100, then click-and-drag the tool from the top of your image, stopping about half way down. Now, Right-click on the Graduated Filter edit pin and choose **Duplicate** to double-up this effect in the exact same place. Duplicate that pin two or three more times until it's really blurry and out of focus up there, with a fairly abrupt change to clear at the bottom. Then, click on New at the top of the Graduated Filter panel, and do this again, but from the bottom of your image going upward, leaving just a thin clear area between this new Graduated Filter and the one coming down from the top. So, you have a really blurry top, and really blurry bottom, and a clear area in the middle that looks like a tiny town (as seen above).

How Do I... Move Brush Edits (and Why)?

To move an edit pin (created when you use the Adjustment Brush, or Graduated or Radial Filter), just click on it and drag it to a new location, and it will retain its original shape. So, why would you ever want to do this? It can save a bunch of time. For example, in the images above, my subject is sitting in a chair. I clicked on the first shot I wanted to edit, then I selected the rest of the photos where she's sitting in a chair. Then, I turned on Auto Sync at the bottom of the right side Panels area (see page 97), so that as I make edits to this image, the exact same edits will be made to all the other selected images. I took the Adjustment Brush, double-clicked on the word "Effect" to reset all the sliders to zero, then I increased the Exposure to 0.71 and painted over her face and part of her hair to brighten those areas. Since I had Auto Sync turned on, it brightened that exact same spot in each of the other frames. The problem is, my subject didn't stay perfectly still—she moved a bit in each frame—so all my edits are either a little or a lot off. No problem. First, I deselected all the images **(Command-D [PC: Ctrl-D])**, then I moved to the first image where the brightening is off (look at the inset above; the brightened area is off to her right—it's the right size, but out of position). Then, I simply clicked on the edit pin and dragged the brightened area right over her face—two seconds and done. On the next photo, I did the same thing—dragged the edit pin right over her face—and then I moved to the next one, and so on. A huge time-saver, especially when you think about how long it would take to individually paint over each photo. It's much quicker and easier to simply drag an existing brush edit right where you want it.

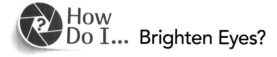

How Do I... Brighten Eyes?

This is a great little trick I learned from pro retoucher (and KelbyOne instructor) Kristina Sherk (from Shark Pixel). Get the Radial Filter tool **(Shift-M)** from the tool-bar beneath the Develop module's Histogram panel, double-click on "Effect" to reset all the sliders to zero, then turn on the Invert checkbox near the bottom of the panel (so the sliders affect what's inside the oval rather than outside it). Now, increase the Exposure amount to around 0.70, and then click-and-drag out an oval over your subject's eye (or even the whole eye socket) to brighten it. You can reshape the oval by clicking-and-dragging any of the four adjustment handles around it, and rotate it by moving your cursor outside the oval and clicking-and-dragging. When it looks good, adjust the Exposure amount so the brightening over the eye looks good. Once you get the oval at the shape and brightness you want over the first eye, Right-click directly on its edit pin and choose **Duplicate** (as seen above) to make another identical oval with the same settings. This duplicate appears right on top of the original oval, so click-and-drag this duplicate edit pin, positioning it over the other eye. *Note:* The red area you see over her left eye here is just showing you a preview of the area that I've masked—you can see a mask preview any time you want by hovering your cursor over an edit pin.

To get rid of a moiré pattern (color banding stripes or weird patterns that appear over clothing, or luggage, or in this case, a guitar strap [notice the pink and blue stripes in the strap, above left?]), get the Adjustment Brush **(K)** from the toolbar beneath the histogram in the Develop module. Then, double-click on the word "Effect" near the top left of the panel to reset all the sliders to zero. Now, near the bottom of the panel, increase the Moiré amount quite a bit, and then paint over the moiré pattern to remove it (as seen in the image above right, where the moiré pattern is now gone).

How Do I... Paint White Balance?

Get the Adjustment Brush **(K)** from the toolbar beneath the histogram in the Develop module. Then, double-click on the word "Effect," near the top left of the panel, to reset all the sliders to zero, and then drag the Temp slider toward whichever color you want to paint with. In the most common instance, you'll probably drag it toward yellow and paint over areas in your image that are in the shade and turned blue because your camera was set to Auto White Balance (like the columns on the left in this cathedral in the Before image above. If I want to remove that blue, I'd move my Temp slider away from blue, toward yellow). Now, just paint over those blue areas (in this case), and then tweak the Temp slider until they are more neutral looking (like in the After image above). Easy peasy.

There's a little thing I do to every portrait, at the very end of my retouching, that might seem subtle, but I think it actually makes a bigger difference than it seems. I get the Adjustment Brush **(K)** from the toolbar beneath the histogram in the Develop module, then double-click on the word "Effect" near the top left of the panel to reset all the sliders to zero. I increase the Exposure amount to around 0.50, and then paint over my subject's entire face. This helps to brighten it a little more than the rest of my subject, and this subtle addition of brightness helps to draw the viewer right where you want them to look. The bonus is it usually makes your subject's face look that much better. Just use a nice, soft, big brush, and make sure the Auto Mask checkbox is turned off near the bottom of the panel, so the brightening is smooth with no gaps.

Chapter 6

How to Create Special Effects

The Easy Way to Get Cool Looks Fast

I've been messing with you a lot in these chapter intros, and there have been things I've said that sounded totally legit, but then just a few sentences later you realize that I made the whole thing up, and I know that hurt you, and I want to make up for it. I want to make up for it by finally telling you the truth about what's in this chapter, and not by hiding behind vague *Star Wars* references or mild inferences that I may have been a tank commander in the Soviet army during a time when we were not that friendly with the Soviet army (so, literally anytime except for about 15 minutes during WWII). Here goes, I'm going all in, straight up on the truth in telling you that the effects in this chapter on special effects are not all that special. This chapter should have just been named "Effects." There, I said it. And, you know what? This whole "Telling the truth, but just for a very brief period" thing feels good. It kinda reminds me of that time when I was second-in-command of a French nuclear-powered attack sub, the FNS *Camembert*, of the Marine Nationale, and we were out doing some strategic deterrence maneuvers near the sea of Roquefort. We were just cruising along, doing about 22 knots, at a depth of around 620 feet, when all of a sudden there was this huge clanging sound like we hit something metal. Well, the commander nearly tossed his raclette and everybody was screaming and sirens were going off, so I yelled to the helmsman, "Surface! Surface!" Then, when we get to the surface, what pops up right next to us with a big ol' gash in her side? That's right, a Russian Navy Typhoon Class sub. Well, everybody was pretty freaked out, and then the Russians popped the hatch on their conning tower, and I saw their commander appear, so I grabbed my binoculars, then my bullhorn, and yelled, "Rhredondunt! Is that you, you ol' dog?" Small world, folks. Small world. By the way, every word of this is true. Je ne voudrais pas mentir, mon ami.

At the top right of the Develop module's Basic panel, click on the words "Black & White." That's the one-click method, but you'll get a fairly flat result. You can choose **Monochrome** from the Profile pop-up menu as a second method, but it's a fairly flat-looking result, too. If you want more choices (and better results), skip those (leave your photo in color) and near the top right of the panel, click on the icon with four little squares to bring up the Profile Browser. Scroll down to the B&W profiles and you'll find 17 different profiles for making a black-and-white conversion, and you'll most likely find a much better starting place there. Just hover your cursor over each of the profiles until you find one you like (you'll see an onscreen preview as you hover over each thumbnail), then click on it to apply that profile. Now, click Close at the top right to close the browser. Scroll down to the B&W panel (it appears when you convert to black and white) and you can use the color sliders to adjust the different tones in the image. I recommend dragging each slider back and forth a few times to see which areas of the image it adjusts, and then use them to tweak the conversion. Now, go back up to the Basic panel. This is where I add lots of contrast, and I drag the Whites slider to the right as far as I can without clipping the highlights and the Blacks slider to the left as far as I can without the shadows turning solid black. I add some Clarity to bring out detail, and my final stop is the Detail panel, where I add a lot of sharpening (I set the amount to around 60 or 70) to finish off the conversion. The Before image on the left above is what you get from just clicking Black & White.

First, in the Develop module, convert your image to B&W (see the previous page for how to do that; you can apply this effect to a color image if you like, but to get the classic duotone look, it's usually applied to a black-and-white image). In the right side Panels area, scroll down to the Split Toning panel. In the Shadows section, at the bottom of the panel, drag the Saturation slider over to around 25 (this brings the color into your black-and-white image), then drag the Hue slider in the Shadows section over between 25 and 35 for a brownish tone (well, that's the range I use anyway but, of course, you can choose any duotone tint you like). Lastly, lower the Saturation slider to somewhere around 15 and that should do the trick. Don't touch the Highlights sliders. Don't touch the Balance slider. Don't touch anything else, 'cause...yer done!

How Do I... Create a Spotlight Effect?

In the Develop module, click on the Radial Filter up in the toolbar (right under the Histogram panel, in the right side Panels area) and then double-click on the word "Effect" in the options panel below it to reset all the sliders to zero. Drag the Exposure slider quite a bit to the left to darken the overall exposure, then at the bottom of the panel, make sure the Invert checkbox is turned off. Now, click in the center of the area where you want your dramatic spotlight to fall and drag outward. Stop dragging at the size you want your spotlight to be. You can increase the Feather amount to make the edges softer and you can make the shape more of an oval, if you like, by clicking on a point at the top, bottom, or sides and just pulling outward (or pushing inward). If it's not exactly where you want it, you can click inside the oval and drag it wherever you like on your image. To rotate the oval, move your cursor just outside the oval and your cursor will change into a two-headed arrow, then just click-and-drag in the direction you want your oval to rotate.

We add vignette effects in a completely different place from where we fix vignetting problems (see, if you don't want a vignette, it's a problem. But, if you add an even darker one then, suddenly, it's cool). You do this in the Effects panel (in the Develop module's right side Panels area) by simply dragging the Post-Crop Vignetting Amount slider to the left (as I did above). If you want your edge darkening to extend farther in toward the center, just drag the Midpoint slider to the left (if you drag it to the right, it moves the darkening up into the corners and away from the center). Keep the Style set to **Highlight Priority** for the best look. Lastly, if you want something more subtle than this—so subtle most folks won't even realize you applied a vignette at all, but if you toggled it on/off you'd see there's actually a fairly significant difference (which is why I love this next setting)—then use –11 for your Amount. It definitely does the job, but nobody will realize you added a vignette.

How Do I... Make an HDR Image?

In the Library module, select the bracketed images you want to combine into a single HDR (High Dynamic Range) image. (*Tip:* This feature works best using just two images: your two stops underexposed and your two stops overexposed images. You can ignore the normal exposure and any other exposures you took, as well.) Now, go under the Photo menu, under Photo Merge, choose **HDR**, and the HDR Merge Preview dialog will appear, showing you a preview of your merged HDR image. If you hand-held the multiple exposures, turn on the Auto Align checkbox and it will try to align the images for you (it does a pretty amazing job). Turn on the Auto Settings checkbox to apply an automatic toning, so it looks better (it usually does with HDR images like this, but not always. Luckily, you see a preview, so if it doesn't look good, turn it off). If you see any ghosting (where something or someone moved during your exposures), choose the Deghost Amount that fits the amount of motion (click on each to see which one looks best). If you turn on the Create Stack checkbox, when you merge your HDR, it will automatically stack the bracketed images that created it, along with the final HDR (see page 37 for more on stacking). When it looks good to you, hit the Merge button and it processes the images at full resolution. When it's done, a new file will appear next to your originally selected images, with HDR.dng at the end of its name. Finally, finish off the image using the Develop module controls. (*Tip:* HDR shots usually like a little bit of Clarity. Well, mine do, anyway.) ;-)

In the Library module, select the images you want to combine into a single panoramic image. Go under the Photo menu, under Photo Merge, choose **Panorama**, and the Panorama Merge Preview dialog appears, showing you a preview of your stitched image. It chooses what style of panorama stitching it thinks best fits the image, and it usually does a really good job, but if for some reason it doesn't, or you don't like the results, click on each of the three projections (Spherical, Cylindrical, and Perspective) to see which one looks good to you. There's an Auto Crop check-box, which automatically crops your photo to remove any white gaps around the edges, which were created when your pano was stitched (you'll almost always have these). The downside of Auto Crop is that your final image winds up being smaller because you cropped away those white areas. That's why I love the Boundary Warp feature. Just drag this slider all the way to the right and, like magic, it fills in those gaps for you, and it does a pretty amazing job. If you turn on the Create Stack check-box, when you merge your pano, it will automatically stack the images you used to create it, along with the final pano (see page 37 for more on stacking). When you're done, click the Merge button, and it creates the full-resolution version in the background, so you can work on something else. When it's finished, it will appear alongside the images you chose for your pano, and if the images you started with were RAW images, the result is a panoramic image that is also a RAW .dng image, which is pretty amazing if you think about it.

This is a recipe that works pretty well to create the trendy high-contrast portrait look. To be sure we're applying the effect to just our subject and not the background, it starts with getting the Adjustment Brush **(K)** from the toolbar below the histogram, in the Develop module's right side Panels area, and double-clicking on the word "Effect" near the top of the tool options to reset all the sliders to zero. Now, increase the Contrast (here, I increased it to 27), then open up the Shadows a bit (here, I increased them to 66), and then paint over just your subject's hair and skin. The big things are the next two: (1) increase the Clarity quite a bit (it helps bring out the texture, and here I dragged it over to 30), and then (2) drag the Saturation slider to the left (I dragged it over to –36) to desaturate your subject a bit (as seen above, in the After on the right). The settings I showed you here are for this particular image (I also ended up decreasing the Highlights and the Whites), but even if the numbers change a little bit for your image, the sliders are the same (add contrast, shadows, clarity, and desaturate a bit).

In the Develop module's Presets panel, in the left side Panels area, you'll see sets of pre-designed, one-click effects put there by Adobe. To see a preview of how any of these would look applied to your image, move your cursor over a preset to get an on-screen preview. When you see one that looks good, click on it, and it applies that look (here, I applied the Soft Mist preset to take the edge off this very sharp image). One thing you need to know about presets is that all they do is move Lightroom's sliders to a preset location to create a particular look. They don't do things you couldn't do yourself if you knew which sliders to drag. To understand why that matters, try this: apply the Aged Photo preset under Classic – Color Presets, then look at the Basic panel sliders and you'll see it adjusts the white balance (Temp and Tint), Blacks, Saturation, and Vibrance. Now, click the next one down—Bleach Bypass— and the sliders will change. So, can you not stack one preset on top of another? You can, as long as it doesn't affect the sliders your first preset used. For example, if you applied the Aged Photo preset, you could then apply the Grain – Heavy preset (under Classic – Effects) because it only uses the Grain sliders in the Effects panel and leaves the Basic panel's sliders untouched. Presets are different than creative profiles (see page 150) because those "looks" don't move your sliders at all—they're completely independent. So, you could apply a creative profile to get a base look, then come here and apply any preset on top of it without a problem.

Once you have a look in place that you like, to save it as a one-click preset (so you can use it again anytime, including when your images are being imported), go to the Presets panel, in the Develop module's left side Panels area, click the little + (plus sign) button on the right side of the panel header, and choose **Create Preset**, which brings up the New Develop Preset dialog you see above. Make sure just the checkboxes beside the sliders you adjusted to get your look are turned on, give your preset a name, then click the Create button and your preset is saved (you'll find your new preset at the bottom of the Presets panel, under User Presets, and in the Develop Settings pop-up menu, in the Import window's Apply During Import panel [see page 8, in Chapter 1]).

How Do I... Get Presets I Downloaded from the Web into Lightroom?

Go to the Presets panel, in the Develop module's left side Panels area, click the little + (plus sign) button on the right side of the panel header, and choose **Import Presets** (as shown above). Now just navigate your way to the preset you downloaded, click the Import button, and that preset will appear in your User Presets set.

If you're using an older computer, or a low-powered laptop, you might notice a speed hit when you hover your cursor over presets in the Presets panel because it takes a lot of "juice" to quickly display a preview of all those different effects right on your image itself. If you notice that speed hit, go to the Preferences (under the Lightroom [PC: Edit] menu), click on the Performance tab, and turn off the Enable Hover Preview of Presets in Loupe checkbox. That turns off the full-size preset preview and gives you back that lost performance. Now, when you hover your cursor over a preset, you'll only see a preview of it on the small thumbnail in the Navigator panel (at the top of the left side Panels area), not on the image in the Preview area. Again, only turn this off if you notice your performance getting sluggish when you hover over a preset.

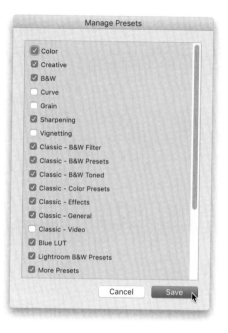

Go to the Presets panel, in the Develop module's left side Panels area, click the + (plus sign) button on the right side of the panel header, and choose **Manage Presets** to bring up the Manage Presets dialog you see above. Turn off the checkbox beside any group of presets you want hidden from view in the Presets panel, click the Save button, and now those presets are hidden. To bring them back at any time, go to the Manage Presets dialog and turn those checkboxes back on.

How Do I... Create "Looks" Using Creative Profiles?

Start by going near the top right of the Basic panel, in the Develop module's right side Panels area, and click on the icon with four little squares to bring up the Profile Browser. When the browser appears, scroll down to either the Artistic, B&W, Modern, or Vintage profiles. Hover your cursor over any of the profiles and you'll get an on-screen preview of how that profile would look if you chose it. (*Tip:* If you want to temporarily turn off the onscreen preview, just press-and-hold the Option [PC: Alt] key.) To choose one you like, just click on it and it's applied to the photo (as seen here, where I scrolled down to the Modern set of creative profiles and clicked on the Modern 03 profile).

How Do I... Create Wet Streets?

Get the Adjustment Brush **(K)** from the toolbar below the histogram, in the Develop module's right side Panels area, double-click on the word "Effect" near the top left of the panel options to reset all the sliders to zero, then drag the Contrast slider over to 100 and the Clarity slider over to 100. Now, paint over a street and it'll look wet. If you want the street to look even wetter, click the New button up at the top right of the panel, then paint over the street again, and it doubles-up the effect (as seen here at right).

Chapter 7

How to Save Your Images

Using Lightroom's Export

Getting photos into Lightroom is easy. Editing them is easy. Doing slide shows is…well… let's skip that one for now. Printing is easy. Organizing is easy. You know what's not easy? Finding the Save menu command inside of Lightroom. Yeah, you know, you've made some edits to your image in the Develop module and want to save those changes, so you go under the File menu to look for Save, but it's just not there. You see, Lightroom is the "Hotel California" of applications, in that you can edit any time you like, but you can never have your image actually leave Lightroom—it's in here for life. It's like the "pen" (well, at least that's what my cellmate called it when we were thrown in Leavenworth for trying to take a tilt-rotor V-22 Osprey out for a joyride with the admiral's daughter). Anyway, while it seems that not having a Save command would mean your images can never leave Lightroom, that's just not the case. Adobe just uses a different word for it. Go under the File menu, under Jailbreak, and choose Breakout, Spontaneous Parole, or Bust Out. This brings up the Warden dialog, where you choose where you want your file saved (your choices are: a halfway house or your ex-boyfriend's/ex-girlfriend's house). You think I'm making this stuff up? Okay, I am, but I don't want you to think I am, because then you'll stop buying my books, and then I won't have any money to bribe the prison guards to keep my Creative Cloud subscription active. Before CC came out, they were fine taking a pack of cigarettes, but if you try to bribe them now with some smokes, they'll make you get a Lightroom 4 tattoo across your knuckles. That's the last thing you want in the "cooler."

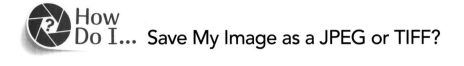

Click on the image(s) you want to save as a JPEG, TIFF, etc. and then press **Command-Shift-E (PC: Ctrl-Shift-E)** to bring up the Export dialog (by the way, Lightroom's word for "Save" is "Export," so think of it as though you're "exporting" your image outside of Lightroom). Besides using that keyboard shortcut, you can also go to the bottom of the left side Panels area in the Library module and click on the Export button. Once the Export dialog is open, from the Export To pop-up menu at the top, choose where you want this saved image to go (do you want it saved on your hard drive? For email? Go "old school" and burn it to a CD or DVD? Maybe you could make a VHS tape while you're at it? Okay, sorry, that was mean). Anyway, that's the first item on your agenda—choose what you're going to do with it—then start down through the rest of the dialog, answering everything from where on your hard drive you want it saved (provided you chose Hard Drive from that pop-up menu), to which file format you want it saved in (JPEG, TIFF, PSD [Photoshop's native format], or DNG [Adobe's digital negative format]), or if you just want to export the original file as-is (perhaps you want to just take a RAW file out of Lightroom). Adobe put some presets over on the left to get you going (I think of them as starting points—you click one and it gets you close to what you want, then you just change or turn on/off any options you want/don't want). When you're done, click the Export button in the bottom-right corner, and you'll see an export progress bar appear in the Activity Center (in the top-left corner of Lightroom), so you'll know when it's done exporting.

How Do I... Save Again with the Same Settings?

Go under the File menu and choose **Export with Previous** (or press **Command-Option-Shift-E [PC: Ctrl-Alt-Shift-E]**). The Export dialog won't appear—it just immediately exports (saves) your image—because when you choose this, you're saying to Lightroom, "Just use the same settings I used before." This is an incredibly handy feature.

To save your Export settings as a preset (so you don't have to type everything in from scratch every time you want to save an image), in the Export dialog, put all your settings in place first, then click the Add button at the bottom of the presets on the left. This brings up a small dialog (shown in the inset above) where you can name your preset and choose where to save it (by default, it saves under User Presets. And, you can save more than one—as you can see here, I have three presets saved under my User Presets). Now, next time you want to export, you can use this preset and save a ton of time. Better yet, now when you want to export an image, you can just Right-click on its thumbnail and, from the pop-up menu, under **Export**, you'll see all the export presets you can choose. That way, you can skip seeing the Export dialog altogether.

In the Export dialog (**Command-Shift-E [PC: Ctrl-Shift-E]**), go to the Image Sizing section, turn on the Resize to Fit checkbox, then from the pop-up menu to the right, choose how you want to resize your image(s) (you can do everything from choosing just the long edge or short edge dimensions, to the number of megapixels you want it exported at, to a percentage, like having the saved image be 25% of the size of the original). Once you make your choice from this pop-up menu, the appropriate set of options for your choice will appear so you can make your selections. Also, you can choose your unit of measure—inches, pixels, or centimeters—from the pop-up menu to the right of the height field. Of course, none of this kicks in until you actually hit the Export button (and just remember not to worry—you're only resizing a copy of the image you are exporting, you are not resizing the original file, so no harm will come to your original file by choosing to resize when you export).

This is another option you'll see as you scroll through the options in the Export dialog **(Command-Shift-E [PC: Ctrl-Shift-E])**, so go to the Output Sharpening section and turn on the Sharpen For checkbox. Once you turn that on, you need to tell it where this image is going to go (onscreen [on the internet, or in a slide show, or just to show on your mobile device or computer], or in print on glossy or matte paper). You choose this so it applies the right amount of sharpening automatically, but that amount is based on your next choice—how sharp you want that final image. There are three choices for Amount: Low, Standard, and High. Unfortunately, there's no preview of how this sharpening is going to look, so you're kinda "flying blind" on this, but you can always do a test—export an image and then open it on your computer to see how the sharpening looks. Hey, it's worth a shot.

How
Do I... Limit How Much Info I Include in the Saved File?

In the Export dialog (**Command-Shift-E [PC: Ctrl-Shift-E]**), scroll down to the Meta-data section, and choose how much (or how little) camera data and personal info you want included in your saved file because, by default, it pretty much includes everything—from the make and model of your camera (and perhaps its serial number), to the date, time, and even GPS information of where it was taken. If that's more information than you need to share, you might want to consider a preset that limits that data, like Copyright Only, or the one I prefer, which is Copyright & Contact Info Only (it only does so much good if someone sees that your image is copyrighted, but there's no contact info for you).

How Do I... Add a Watermark to My Images?

Scroll down in the Export dialog **(Command-Shift-E [PC: Ctrl-Shift-E])** to the Watermarking section, and turn on the Watermark checkbox. From the pop-up menu to the right, choose **Edit Watermarks** to bring up the Watermark Editor dialog where you can create and apply your watermark. If you have a logo you want to use as your watermark, then for the Watermark Style at the top right, click on the Graphic radio button, then click on the Choose button right below in the Image Options section, and find your logo (which is what I did here). Once it appears, position it over the image using the Anchor grid of nine dots in the Watermark Effects section. That'll get it close to where you want it, and then you can use the Inset Horizontal and Vertical sliders to put it right where you want it. There's a Size slider, two rotate buttons, and an Opacity slider (if you want your logo to be see-through) in this section, as well. If you want a text watermark, go back up and click on the Text radio button for the Watermark Style. Now, just type in your text in the field below the preview area (by default, it uses the name you registered the software in, but you can just highlight that and type in anything you like), and then in the Text Options section, choose your font options, as well as if you want to add a drop shadow to help it stand out. When you're done with your watermark (graphic or text), you can save it so you don't have to create it again: from the pop-up menu, in the top-left corner of the dialog, choose **Save Current Settings as New Preset** and give it a name. Now, it will appear as a choice in the Export dialog's Watermark pop-up menu when you turn on the Watermark checkbox.

At the bottom of the Export dialog **(Command-Shift-E [PC: Ctrl-Shift-E])** is the Post-Processing section, which is where you choose what happens to your image after it's saved. Do Nothing means just that. If you want to open it in another application, including an email application or another editing app, choose **Open in Other Application** (as shown above). The Choose button below becomes active, and you can then choose the application you want (it brings up a standard Open dialog, where you can navigate to the application you want, click on it, then click Choose, and that app will now be added to a pop-up menu to the left of the Choose button).

How Do I... Email a Photo from within Lightroom?

In the Library module, just select your photo(s), then go under the File menu and choose **Email Photo** (as shown above).This brings up Lightroom's email dialog, with your default mail application chosen (in the From pop-up menu) as the vehicle that will actually send the photo. In this dialog, you enter the email address of the person you want to send the image to, you can copy someone by adding them in the Cc field, include a subject line, and from the pop-up menu at the bottom left, you can choose the size and quality you'd like for your emailed photo.

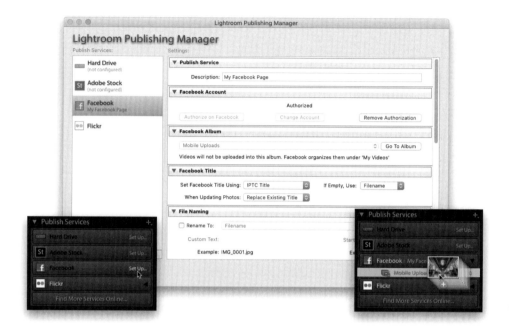

Lightroom Classic lets you do a "one-click" publish to some of the most popular online photo sharing sites, including Facebook, Flickr, Adobe Stock, and others, and it comes with presets for some already in place—you just have to basically authorize these services to accept your photos directly from Lightroom. To do that, in the Library module, go to the Publish Services panel (in the left side Panels area) and click on the Set Up button for the service you want (as seen in the inset above left) to bring up the Publishing Manager (seen above center). This is where you authorize the sharing site (in the example above, my Facebook page) to accept images you choose to send there directly from Lightroom. It'll ask you which album you want them to go into (well, it does for Facebook anyway), along with some other simple stuff, and when you're done, just click the Save button. Now it's configured and ready to go. To actually publish (send) an image to your Facebook page from Lightroom, just click-and-drag the image directly to that album—it'll appear under Facebook in the Publish Services panel (as seen in the inset above right, where I'm dragging nine images that I want published directly to my Facebook page).

In the File Settings section of the Export dialog **(Command-Shift-E [PC: Ctrl-Shift-E])**, you get to choose your file type (JPEG, TIFF, and so on), but it's making the right Color Space choice that determines if the colors of your image look pretty much like you see here in Lightroom, or whether they'll be pretty much messed up. I'll make it simple: choose **sRGB** for posting images to the web. They'll look the closest by far to what you're seeing onscreen in Lightroom.

In the Library module, click on your RAW image, then under Metadata, choose **Save Metadata to File** (or just press **Command-S [PC: Ctrl-S]**). This saves an XMP file (called a "sidecar"), along with your exported original RAW file (as seen in the inset above), and this XMP file contains all the edits you made to this image in Lightroom. If you were to give these two files to someone else and they opened this RAW image in their copy of Lightroom (or in an application that supports XMP data, like Adobe Bridge or Photoshop, for example), that RAW image would reflect the same settings you applied to it in Lightroom. For other applications outside Adobe's own, they may honor all the changes stored in the XMP sidecar file, or just the basic metadata stuff, like embedded keywords, captions, and copyright data. Again, it just depends on the application. This whole XMP thing is also how you're able to make edits to your RAW photos in Lightroom on your laptop, and then copy those RAW photos over to your main computer, and it still sees all the edits you made to those RAW images.

Chapter 8

How to Make Photo Books

Using Lightroom's Built-In Book Module

I wanted to name this chapter "Making Beautiful Photo Books," but then I realized that some people might make a photo book of insects, or macro shots of insects, or worse yet, really close-up macro shots of gross insects, so I left the beautiful part out, because I gotta tell ya, if I see a book of insect shots, I'm outta there. I'd rather look at a photo book called "Extreme Public Porta-Potty Catastrophes" than to see even one page of insects up close. Here's why: even though an extreme porta-potty meltdown certainly doesn't look pleasing, their real impact is when you're there in person on the business end of the full aromatic experience—at that point, it's a 4D experience that can make you pass out in seconds (I have run screaming from them on more than one occasion, yelling "I will pay anyone to chop off my entire nose right now!"). But, again, that's in person. I might look at just a photo and think, "Man, now that is nasty! I'm so glad I'm not there!" But when I see an insect photo—especially a macro shot— I freak out like I'm in a porta-potty at high noon, outside of Newark, on a hot July day, with the outdoor normal relative humidity at like 97%, just as a fully-loaded 2007 Freightliner tractor-trailer rig accidentally backs into the porta-potty, and I realize that the entire unit is about to flip over on its side, if not upside down, and the door to the odoriferous sweatbox is now jammed shut by the force of the impact. That is how much I do not like seeing super-icky insects up close (or at a distance) in any kind of photo book, and in fact, if you are a photographer that shoots that kind of skin-crawling creepy stuff, I suggest you skip this chapter. Maybe the Slide Show chapter, too.

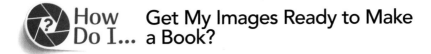

How Do I... Get My Images Ready to Make a Book?

Before you begin your book, put all your final images into a collection (see page 20 in Chapter 2 for more on this). These should be "final" images, meaning they're cropped, sharpened, edited—you name it. Put 'em all in one collection, and then click on Book up in the taskbar across the top of Lightroom's window, 'cause you're ready to go!

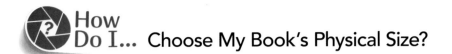

How Do I... Choose My Book's Physical Size?

At the top of the Book module's right side Panels area is the Book Settings panel, and near the top of that panel is the Size pop-up menu (seen above left), which has the standard sizes supported by Blurb.com. Directly below that, you get to choose the Cover style (shown above right). The Softcover choice is actually better looking than you'd think (it's the one I make the most, by far). The Hardcover Dust Jacket option is more like you'd see for a coffee table book, where there's a separately printed, outside glossy cover with flaps that tuck in the front and back. But, don't worry, even if the cover gets torn, or you lose it, etc., the hard cover under it has the same cover image and text printed on it, as well. Finally, the Hardcover Image Wrap option has your image printed right on the cover (picture the dust jacket version without the dust jacket).

How Do I... Have Lightroom Lay Out My Book for Me?

Right under the Book Settings panel (in the right side Panels area) is the Auto Layout panel. It doesn't look like much—just a single pop-up menu and a couple buttons. Click on the Preset pop-up menu and you'll get a list of page layout presets (put there by Adobe, along with ones you create yourself). For example, the one named Left Blank, Right One Photo will create a book with every left page blank (duh), and every right page will automatically be filled with a single photo that fills the page to the side edges, as seen above (yes, it's a pretty darn boring layout, but we'll create our own later). The images appear in the order they appear in the collection you created, with the first image appearing on the cover and page 1, the second image on page 3 (remember, the second page is blank), and so on. If this seems kinda lame, it's only because the presets are lame. When you get some decent looking layouts and create your own presets, this can be a really awesome starting place that gets you 90% of the way there with just one click.

When it comes to changing the order or location of your images, this is pretty much a drag-and-drop situation. For example, you can drag-and-drop images directly from the Filmstrip right into a cell on the pages (those gray photo wells are where you drop images, as seen above, where I'm dragging an image from the Filmstrip to the page on the middle left). You'll see a little green circle with a plus sign in it to let you know you're adding a photo to this page. If you want to swap photos on a spread (swapping the left and right photos), just drag-and-drop one on top of the other, and they swap. To remove an image, click on it and hit the Delete (PC: Backspace) key.

Go to the Auto Layout panel, in the right side Panels area, and from the Preset pop-up menu, choose **Edit Auto Layout Preset** to bring up the Auto Layout Preset Editor dialog you see above. Here, you can choose any layout you want, on the left or right pages separately, from the built-in presets that come with Lightroom. You can choose how many images will appear on each page, what each layout will look like on each side, if they'll have an area to add text, and if the photos will fill the photo cell or fit fully inside it (see page 175 for more on this). If you've created your own custom layouts (see page 174 for more), you can choose those, as well. When you're done choosing what you want to appear on the left page and the right page, it's time to save this as a preset. Just go up to the Preset pop-up menu at the top of the dialog, choose **Save Current Settings as New Preset** (as shown in the inset), and give your preset a name (I usually name mine with something that describes what's on the left side and the right). Now, you can choose these same settings without ever opening the Auto Layout Preset Editor—just choose this preset from the Preset pop-up menu in the Auto Layout panel.

Start by choosing a template from the Preset pop-up menu in the Auto Layout panel (in the right side Panels area). Now, click on a page to make it active, then click on the little black arrow button to open the Modify Page pop-up menu, choose the number of photos you want on the page, and choose a preset thumbnail. Next, click on the bottom-right corner of one of the gray cells, and drag diagonally inward. Once you drag, even just a little bit so you see some white background area, go to the Cell panel (in the right side Panels area), turn off Link All, and now you can either move the Padding sliders (as shown above) to create a custom size for your photo cell, or just drag its edges to the size and shape you want. Do that for each of the photo cells on your custom page.

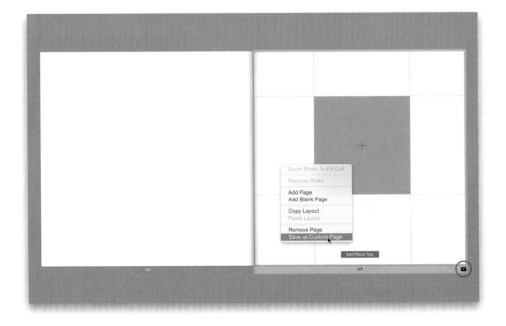

Once you have a custom page set up the way you want it, Right-click anywhere on the page and, from the pop-up menu that appears, choose **Save as Custom Page**. There's no naming it or anything like that—it's just automatically added to the Modify Page pop-up menu, under Custom Pages, where you'll see a small thumbnail of the custom page you've created. You get to this menu by clicking on the little black Modify Page Layout button in the bottom-right corner (circled in red above) of the currently selected page (see page 177 for more on this).

Fit

Fill

✓ Zoom Photo To Fill Cell

Remove Photo

Add Page
Add Blank Page

Copy Layout
Paste Layout

Remove Page
Save as Custom Page

By default, your image will fit inside each photo cell proportionally, which usually means a lot of white space above and below your image inside the photo cell shape (as seen above left). If you want to have your image fill the photo cell (which is what I usually do), just Right-click on your image and choose **Zoom Photo To Fill Cell** (you can also use the Zoom slider that appears over your image when you click on it). If you're using the Auto Layout feature, when you create a custom layout in the Auto Layout Preset Editor, you'll have the option to have your images Fit or Fill the photo cell (you choose this from the Zoom Photos To pop-up menus, seen back on page 172).

Go to the Page panel (in the right side Panels area) and, at the top, turn on the Page Numbers checkbox. You can then choose where you want the page numbers to appear on the page from the pop-up menu to the right (here, I chose Bottom Corner). Also, you can highlight a page number on a page and change its font, size, and style in the Type panel (also in the right side Panels area). If you want to hide the page number for a particular page, just Right-click on the page and choose **Hide Page Number**.

Click on a page and a yellow highlight will appear around it, and in the bottom-right corner you'll see a black arrow button. Click on that button and the Modify Page pop-up menu appears (shown here). Start by clicking on how many photos you want to appear on the page and the templates appear below in a scrolling list, showing a thumbnail of each layout. To apply any layout, just click on it. The option at the very top, Favorites, is all the ones you picked as favorites from Adobe's built-in templates (you can make any of those thumbnails a favorite by Right-clicking on a thumbnail and choosing **Add Layout To Favorites**). Custom Pages, also near the top, are pages you created from scratch and saved to that set (see pages 173–174).

Go to the Background panel (in the right side Panels area), and then go down to the Filmstrip and drag-and-drop the photo you want as your page background onto the background image well, in the middle of the panel (as shown above). If you just want this background to appear behind the page you're working on (rather than appearing on every page in the book), turn off the Apply Background Globally checkbox (shown circled above). Once your background image appears behind your photo, you can control the opacity of the image using the Opacity slider.

To use Lightroom's built-in page background graphics, go to the Background panel (in the right side Panels area), click on the little down-facing arrow to the right of the background image well, and a pop-up menu appears with different sets of background graphics for travel and wedding-style books (along with any images you've used for backgrounds under the Photos set at the top). Once you have a graphic in place, you can change its opacity using the Opacity slider, and even change the color by clicking on the color swatch to the right of the Graphic checkbox (just click on that color swatch and the color picker appears. Click-and-drag the HEX slider on the far right up to the top, and now you can choose from a wide range of colors. Click your cursor inside the large gradient rectangle and your cursor changes into an eye-dropper, so you can pick your color. Also, if you click-and-hold with the eyedropper, and keep holding down the mouse button, you can drag it outside the picker and over onto your image to choose a color from within the image itself, so your background graphic's color perfectly matches the image on the page).

How Do I... Change the Background Color?

Click on the page you want to change the background color on, then go to the Background panel (in the right side Panels area) and turn on the Background Color checkbox. Next, click on the color swatch that appears to the right of that checkbox to bring up the color picker where you can choose your background color (by default, it shows white, black, and some popular shades of gray as little one-click swatches, but if you click-and-drag the HEX slider, over on the far right, up toward the top, the gradient in the middle changes from blacks, whites, and grays into a color gradient). Also, if you want to change the background of just one particular page (like I did here), turn off the Apply Background Globally checkbox at the top of the Background panel or it will change all the pages in your book to that color (unless, of course, that's what you want to do).

How Do I... Add a Caption under My Picture?

Click on a page and you'll see a button appear below the photo that says: "Add Photo Text." Click that button and a text field appears below your image (as seen above), where you can enter a photo caption. If you go to the top of the Text panel (shown above right, on top), you'll see a Photo Text pop-up menu which gives you options for your caption, like automatically pulling EXIF data to use as your caption (stuff like your f-stop, shutter speed, camera make and model, lens choice, etc.). If you don't want any of that auto stuff pulled in as your caption, you can just click in that text field below your photo and start typing. In the middle of the Text panel, you can change the location of your caption. By default, it appears below your image, but you can click the Above button so it appears above your image, or Over to have your caption appear over your image. Lastly, there's an Offset slider here, which lets you control how close to (or far away from) your image your caption appears. Once you've typed in your caption, highlight your text, then go to the Type panel (shown above right, on bottom) to choose your caption's font, size, and/or style (like italic, bold, etc., as seen here, where I chose the font Minion Pro Italic at a 10-point size and I clicked the Centered Text Alignment button at the bottom of the panel).

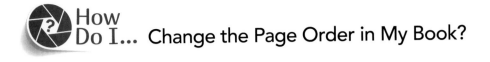

How Do I... Change the Page Order in My Book?

To move a two-page spread to a different location in your book, just click on either the left or right page, then press-and-hold the Command (PC: Ctrl) key, click on the other page, and both pages will be selected (highlighted with a yellow tab going across the bottom of the spread, as seen above). Now, just click directly on that yellow tab at the bottom and drag this spread wherever you want in your book. When you drag it where you want, you'll see a thin vertical bar appear between spreads letting you know where the spread you're moving will appear in the book. If you just want to swap one page (like swapping the left and right pages), simply click on either page, then click on that yellow tab at the bottom of the selected page, and drag it over to the other page in the spread, and they swap.

How Do I... See an Overview of My Entire Book?

If you're looking at a spread or single page, just press **Command-E (PC: Ctrl-E)** to jump to Multi-Page view. Next, press **Shift-Tab** to hide all your panels, so all you see are your pages, then drag the Thumbnail slider (at the bottom-right corner) all the way over to the left to make your thumbnails small enough to see a lot, if not all, of your book onscreen at one time. If all of it can't fit onscreen at the same time, you'll be able to scroll down to see any pages that couldn't fit.

First, click directly on the page you want to remove from your book, then Right-click anywhere on the page and, from the pop-up menu that appears, choose **Remove Page** (as seen here). If you want to remove multiple pages, select them all first (while pressing-and-holding the Command [PC: Ctrl] key), and do the same thing.

Click directly on the image you want to edit (as shown in the inset above), then press the letter **D** to take that image over to the Develop module. Edit it as you would any other photo there, then press **Command-Option-4 (PC: Ctrl-Alt-4)** to jump back to the Book module, and your photo will update automatically to show the edits you made.

Click on a page in your book, then click on the black button with the down-facing arrow in the bottom-right corner of the page (down in the yellow highlighted area) and, in the Modify Page pop-up menu, click on **Two-Page Spreads** to bring up a thumbnail list of two-page spread templates (as seen above). Just click on the layout you want and it applies it to your page, which usually means having it add a blank page to your book because you clicked on one page, but you just added a two-page spread, so somethin's gotta give. Go look in your Multi-Page view **(Command-E [PC: Ctrl-E])** and see if you have an extra page sneaking around in there now right next to where you added your new spread. Depending on where you added it in the book, heck, it could add two pages. Well, at least now ya know.

How Do I... Customize My Cover?

The front cover of your book is treated like a two-page spread (not two separate pages, like the rest of the book), but it does have a bunch of templates you can choose from—just click on the cover, then click on the little black button with the down-facing arrow, in the bottom-right corner, and the Modify Cover pop-up menu with cover templates appears. Click on the one you want and it applies it. If you use the default template (like I did here), it lets you put one photo on the front and one on the back (which I shrunk down in size, using the trick I showed you for how to create a custom page on page 173). Also, all of these templates have some text ready to go, just be sure to turn on the Photo Text checkbox in the Text panel (as seen in the inset above), in the right side Panels area. I also ended up changing the background color to black, here, in the Background panel.

187

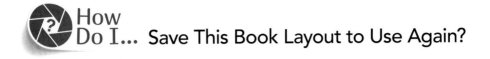

How Do I... Save This Book Layout to Use Again?

Once you're done, go up to the top-right corner of Multi-Page view and click on the Create Saved Book button (shown circled above). That way, if you want to print this same book again some time in the future, it will keep not only this layout, but the same photos in the same order, so you don't have to rebuild it from scratch. When you create a saved book like this, it creates a new collection just for this book, but its icon looks like a book, so you can easily see the difference between a regular collection and this book collection (as seen in the inset above—take a look, for example, at the icon for the NYC collection set versus the book icon for New York Book).

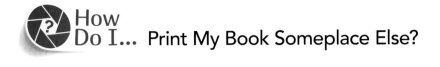

How Do I... Print My Book Someplace Else?

If you want to have your photo book printed someplace other than the default choice of Blurb.com, you can export it in PDF format, ready for print, and deliver that to your photo lab—just click on the Export Book to PDF button at the bottom of the left side Panels area. Of course, before you do that, I'd contact the photo lab directly and ask them if they can take a PDF from Lightroom, and (this is important) if they can make a book in the same size as you chose from the Size pop-up menu (in the Book Settings panel). Those are Blurb's standard sizes and your lab might not be able to print books at Blurb's sizes, so it really pays to check before you upload your PDF file to them.

No Logo—$30.76
Logo—$25.41

Just let Blurb put their small gray logo on the bottom of the last page of your book, and they will give you a full 20% off your book. Can this be right? Oh, it be right! You turn the Blurb logo on/off in the Book Settings panel (at the top of the right side Panels area) from the Logo Page pop-up menu (shown above). Choose to show their logo and save some bucks. The choice is yours.

How Do I... Send My Book Off to Print?

When you're happy with your entire book layout and ready to send it off to be print-ed, just click the Send Book to Blurb button at the bottom of the right side Panels area. Once you sign in (yes, you'll need to create a new account with Blurb—it's free. Well, the account is, the book isn't), you'll enter your book info, then it com-piles the book into a format that works for Blurb, and uploads it to Blurb's website. You'll then choose how many copies you want printed, and whether you want to make the book available for sale in Blurb.com's online bookstore. Once you've made your choices, in just a few days, your printed photo book will arrive.

Chapter 9

How to Make Awesome Slide Shows

Just Don't Put Any Emphasis on the Word "Awesome"

There are parts of Lightroom that get used to death, like the Library and Develop modules, and then there are parts that…well…get used occasionally, but only because: (a) you don't have any other possible option available to you, or (b) you are admittedly too lazy to export your images from Lightroom into any other program on earth that makes slide shows, and therefore your only option is to make one right within Lightroom. Now, you may be asking yourself: "Is he kidding? Is the Slideshow module in Lightroom really all that bad?" Those are questions that can only be asked by someone who has never used it because if you had, you would simply skip over this chapter, because the rest of Lightroom, with the possible exception of the Web module, is actually really good. So, what happened to the Slideshow module that has made it so spartan? So clunky? So unused? So nearly abandoned by Adobe? This is a good question. I can only imagine that when they originally developed Lightroom, a slide show feature was in the initial wish list of features, but they kind of forgot about it until the last minute and just "went with what they had ready." When Lightroom 1.0 came out in 2007, it had a lame slide show feature that is nearly identical to the one we have today, save for a few small, minor improvements. You know what else came out in 2007? The iPhone. Back then, it had a very small 3.5" screen, there were no downloadable apps, and no App Store whatsoever. The "big capacity model" was 8 GB and it had dial-up speed internet. Look at the features of the iPhone today. Now, look back at the minor new features in the Slideshow module in Lightroom since 2007. Back at the iPhone. Now back at Slideshow. See, I wasn't kidding with this one, was I?

There are two things you need to do to get started: (1) put all the images you want in your slide show into a collection, and then (2) go to the Slideshow module, then to the Template Browser panel (in the left side Panels area), and click on one of the predesigned templates as your starting place (as you hover your cursor over any template, a preview of that slide show layout appears in the Preview panel, at the top of the left side Panels area). I say "starting place" because none of them are particularly good looking (here, I went with the Crop To Fill template, which isn't awesome but, like I said, it's a starting place), so choose the one that looks the closest to something you might actually want to use.

How Do I... Make My Own Custom Template?

In the Template Browser (in the Slideshow module's left side Panels area), click on a template to get started (I started here with the one I used on the previous page, Crop To Fill) and use the panels on the right side to change, reposition, and turn on/off things you want (or don't want) to appear on your slide. For example, the first thing I wanted to do here was to customize my slide layout and add space all the way around the image, so I went to the Layout panel and dragged the sliders to the right to add 68 pixels of space on each side, the top, and the bottom (click Link All to unlink the guides, if you want to move them individually). I actually wanted white space around my image (not a black background), so next I went down to the Backdrop panel, turned on the Background Color checkbox (which, by default, adds a light gray color to your background), and then I clicked on the color swatch to the right to bring up the Background Color Picker where I clicked on white. Lastly, I went up to the Options panel (seen above right) and turned on the Stroke Border checkbox and gave it a good thick black border. I also turned on the Cast Shadow checkbox, raising the Radius amount to make the shadow really soft, but leaving the Opacity amount so that it's really subtle. Once you have yours looking how you like it, go over to the Template Browser, and click on the + (plus sign) button on the far right of the panel header to save this layout as your own custom template (the New Template dialog is shown in the inset above). Your template will now appear under User Templates in the Template Browser, so it's always just one click away.

How Do I... Add Music to My Slide Show?

Go to the Music panel (near the bottom of the right side Panels area), click on the Turn on Audio switch on the left side of the panel header, then click on the + (plus sign) button at the top right of the panel and a standard Open dialog appears, where you can choose your music track (you can also choose multiple songs to play one after another, and once you've imported them into Lightroom, you can drag-and-drop them into the order you want them to play). The music files have to be in MP3 or AAC (M4A) format to work with Lightroom, which for me means sometimes having to convert an existing track into AAC (M4A) format first. If you have iTunes for Mac or Windows, it can take a song you have in iTunes and make a new version of it in AAC (M4A) format (otherwise, you can download any one of a bunch of free audio converters that'll do the trick). In your iTunes Music library, click on the song you want to use in Lightroom, then go under the File menu, under Convert, and choose **Create AAC Version**. This creates a duplicate of your song in AAC (M4A) format, and that's the one you can use in Lightroom.

How Do I... Sync My Slide Show to Music?

Right below the Music panel, in the right side Panels area, is the Playback panel, and in the Automatic tab, you'll see the Sync Slides to Music checkbox. Turn that on and Lightroom analyzes the music and tries to sync the changing of the slides to changes in the music track, and every once in a while, it actually works. I haven't had that experience myself, but I've heard stories of people having it work for particular songs. I saw an Adobe demo song where it worked really well and, apparently, if you use that same exact song, it'll work but, outside of that song, it's a total roll of the dice. Is there any way to tweak how it syncs or do it manually, so the slides change right when you want them to? Nope. It either somehow changes the slides when you hope it will, or it doesn't (expect the second of the two). Why am I telling you this? Because I don't want you to think you've done something wrong, or be unduly frustrated, when the results of syncing the music is...ummm... let's say "less than ideal."

How Do I... Add Movement to My Slide Show?

Playback ▼

Slideshow Mode

Automatic | Manual

✔ Sync Slides to Music

Slide Length ──●────── 10 sec
Crossfades ──────●── 2.5 sec

Audio Balance
Video ──●────── Music

✔ Pan and Zoom

Low ───●──── High

✔ Repeat Slideshow
☐ Random Order

Quality | Standard | ⬍

To add movement to your slide show, go to the Playback panel (in the right side Panels area) and turn on the Pan and Zoom checkbox. Right below that, you'll find a slider that goes from Low to High (Low means a little movement and High means a lot, so use that slider to choose how much movement you want). Once your slide show starts, Lightroom will move the images from left to right (and right to left), and at the same time, it will zoom in on the images. The two together work pretty well to create movement and the default dissolve effect that happens between slides helps add to the overall effect.

Playback ▼

Slideshow Mode

Automatic | Manual

☐ Sync Slides to Music

Slide Length ——————●——————— 4.0 sec
Crossfades ———————————●——— 3.2 sec

Fit to Music

Audio Balance
Video ———————●——————————— Music

✔ Pan and Zoom

Low ———————●——————————— High

✔ Repeat Slideshow
☐ Random Order

Quality | Standard ▼

Go to the Playback panel (in the right side Panels area) and make sure the Sync
Slides to Music checkbox is turned off. You'll see the Crossfades slider and that lets
you choose how long the fade between two images lasts (the farther you drag it to
the right, the longer it takes).

Weddings
Collection 2
Haze 4
Ireland HDR 86
Reedits 2
White Bal Virt 1

Export PDF... Export Video...

Quality: 90   Width: 1,440
☐ Automatically show full screen   Height: 900
Common sizes: Screen
Notes: Adobe Acrobat transitions use a fixed speed.
Music is not saved in PDF Slideshows.

Video Preset: 640 x 480 (4:3)

Optimized for small handheld devices and web. Compatible with Adobe
Media Player, Apple Quicktime, and Windows Media Player 12.

At the bottom of the Slideshow module's left side Panels area are buttons for exporting your slide show either as a PDF or a video file. Click on either one and it brings up those options for choosing the size you want to save it at. In the case of exporting it as a PDF, there's a quality setting, as well, and an option for the PDF slide show to automatically go full screen when it's launched.

Go to the Playback panel in the right side Panels area, make sure the Sync Slides to Music checkbox is turned off, and then choose how long you want your Crossfades (the dissolve transition between slides) to be. Then, click the Fit to Music button (as seen above). It will do the math for you, based on how many slides you have in your slide show and how long of a crossfade you choose, and it'll automatically choose the proper Slide Length, so your slide show ends when the music ends. If you need your slides onscreen longer than it chooses, lower the length of the Crossfades, and then hit the Fit to Music button again to recalculate.

Go to the Titles panel, in the right side Panels area, and turn on the Intro Screen checkbox (or Ending Screen, whichever you want to create). Turning this on only creates a blank screen at the start (or end) of your slide show, so if you want to add text and create a title slide, then turn on the Add Identity Plate checkbox, as well (as seen above left). To edit the text that will appear on your title slide, click on the little down-facing triangle in the bottom right of the Identity Plate preview window (the checkerboard rectangle) and choose **Edit**, which brings up the Identity Plate Editor (shown above right). Type in your text in the text field, then highlight it and choose a font, size, and style from the pop-up menus below (here, I chose Al Fresco, available at MyFonts.com). On the far right, there's a color swatch that shows the current color. Just click on that swatch to bring up the Colors picker to choose a new color (remember, these changes only affect type you've highlighted first). When you click OK, you'll see your title slide appear onscreen for a few seconds and then it goes away. I have no idea why it does it, but it does. Always has. But, the trick to getting it back onscreen is to just click-and-hold on the Scale slider knob (it controls the size of your text on the Intro screen, even though theoretically you just chose the size in the Identity Plate Editor, right?), which makes your Intro screen visible again, so you can tweak the size. There's no way to change the position of the type on the Intro screen, though—it will always be centered. If you're thinking this all sounds very limiting and weird, just know that you're not alone.

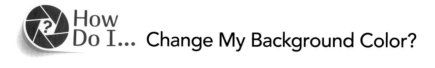

How Do I... Change My Background Color?

Go to the Backdrop panel, in the right side Panels area, and you'll see the Background Color checkbox at the bottom. Click on the color swatch to the right to bring up the Background Color picker, where you can choose any background color you'd like (by default, it's going to look like you can only choose black, white, or shades of gray, but if you click-and-drag the HEX slider on the far right upward, you'll see all the colors appear). Besides a solid color, if you leave the Color Wash checkbox (at the top of the panel) turned on, you'll get a background gradient that graduates from the Color Wash color (you pick this by clicking on its color swatch) to whichever color you have chosen for the Background Color. So, as you can see above, I went from the yellow Color Wash to a blue Background Color. Up near the top of the panel, you can also choose the direction of your gradient by clicking-and-dragging on the Angle dial.

Go to the Backdrop panel, in the right side Panels area, turn off the Color Wash checkbox at the top, then turn on the Background Image checkbox in the middle, and you'll see a small square that says, "Drag background image from filmstrip to here." Do just that, and—blammo—the image you dropped in there becomes the background (as seen above). However, when it comes in, it's "full power" (meaning it's not nicely backscreened behind your image, like the one you see above), so I recommend two things: (1) Change your Background Color to white (as seen here, where I clicked on the Background Color swatch and, in the Background Color picker, I switched the color from black to white. This makes the backscreened effect look much better). And, (2) lower the image's Opacity using the slider right below the Background Image well (I lowered it to 34% here). Now this image will appear behind all the slides in your slide show.

You do this pretty much the same way as you do everything else in Lightroom where there's a layout option—your image fits inside a "cell," and you can change the size of the cell to change the size of your image (since it has to fit inside that cell). You do that by going to the Layout panel (near the top of the right side Panels area) and moving the cell margins using the four sliders (Left, Right, Top, and Bottom). By default, they are linked, so if you move one side, they all move as a unit. If you want to create your own custom layout, start by clicking on Link All to unlink the margins, so now you can move each slider independently. As you move each slider, you'll see your image move and resize, so just move them until you get to the size and position you want.

Go to the Overlays panel, in the right side Panels area, and turn on the Text Overlays checkbox. Now, look down in the toolbar, below the Preview area, and you'll see an ABC button. Click on that button and the Custom Text field appears to the right of it, where you can type in the custom text you want (as seen here), or you can click-and-hold on the words "Custom Text," and a pop-up menu appears where you can choose things like captions or camera data to be automatically pulled from the image's metadata and displayed under it instead (your choice). Once your text is in place, you can choose the Font and Face style in the Text Overlays section of the Overlays panel, along with the color (just click on the color swatch to the right of the Text Overlays checkbox). To resize the text, just click directly on it, and a bounding box will appear around it. Click on a corner and drag outward (or inward) to resize. You can also click-and-drag the entire text block to reposition it, including dragging it right on top of your image.

Go to the Overlays panel (in the right side Panels area) and, at the top, turn on the Identity Plate checkbox. Click on the little down-facing triangle in the bottom-right corner of the Identity Plate preview (the checkerboard rectangle) and choose **Edit**, which brings up the Identity Plate Editor (shown above on the top right). Click on the Use a Graphical Identity Plate radio button, then click the Locate File button, find your logo on your computer, and then click OK to import that logo (the shape of my logo prevents it from fully appearing in the long, thin, horizontal preview area, so that's why you can only see the top of it). Click OK and your logo will appear onscreen. You can click-and-drag it wherever you'd like it, as well as resize it by dragging one of the corner handles, or by using the Scale slider in the Identity Plate section of the Overlays panel. There's also an Opacity slider there if you want to lower the opacity of your logo.

How Do I... Add a Drop Shadow to My Slides?

Go to the Options panel (at the top of the right side Panels area) and turn on the Cast Shadow checkbox (as seen in the inset above). You have four controls: Opacity controls how dark the shadow is; Offset is how far away from the photo the shadow appears; Radius is how large (and soft) the shadow appears; and Angle lets you choose the direction of the shadow. Of course, make sure you choose a Background Color (in the Backdrop panel) that lets the drop shadow be seen (so, a black background is pretty much out, right?).

There are two ways to play your slide show: Clicking the Preview button (at the bottom of the right side Panels area) shows your slide show, surrounded by black, but just within the Preview area where you're building it. This is handy because Lightroom doesn't have to render all your images at full-screen size to do this, so it goes quickly and smoothly (and the music plays, transitions appear, the whole nine yards. It's just a smaller size—a preview size). To pause the Preview slide show, click the Pause button down in the toolbar below the Preview area (as seen above). Clicking the Play button (also at the bottom of the right side Panels area) presents the slide show full-screen size, so you don't see Lightroom at all. To exit this full-screen view, press the Esc key on your keyboard and it returns you to Lightroom. There is no Rewind button, so to start your slide show over, scroll your Filmstrip all the way to the left, click on the first slide, and then start your slide show again. Also, by default, it plays all the images in your collection. If you just want some particular images in your collection to play, select them first down in the Filmstrip, then from the Use pop-up menu in the toolbar, choose **Selected Photos**.

How Do I... Save My Slide Show for Later?

If you want to save this exact slide show, with this particular layout and these images in this order, here's what to do: go up to the top-right corner of the Preview area and click the Create Saved Slideshow button (shown circled here in red. By the way, if you don't see this button up there, just hit the **\[backslash] key** on your keyboard to make it visible). This creates a new collection in the Collections panel (or you can choose to save it inside the original collection, in the Create Slideshow dialog), but it remembers all these attributes, so you're always just one click away. Also, this collection has a different icon, one that looks like a little Play button (as seen in the inset above), so you know at a glance it's a slide show.

If you're previewing or playing your slide show and it stutters a bit or doesn't play as smoothly as it should, you can lower the Quality setting from the Quality pop-up menu at the bottom of the Playback panel (in the right side Panels area). Now, try it again with the lower Draft quality, which doesn't tax the system or need high-resolution rendering to play smoothly. Don't worry, though; this won't affect the final slide show you export from Lightroom—that always stays at full quality. This just affects the quality of your slide show while you're working on it here in Lightroom, so lowering the quality here makes it smoother and faster while you're editing, without messing with the quality of the final product.

Chapter 10

How to Print

Working in the Print Module

Look, I'm trying to stay true to the vision of these chapter intros by starting each one with "How to," and then naming the thing it shows you how to do (in this case, print), but in this case, the subhead (where I break down where we'll be working) is kind of dumb looking ("Working in the Print Module"). I almost want to write the word "duh" at the end of the subhead, so you know that I know it's totally obvious and majorly redundant. This is a side note, but believe it or not, I was in the military when I was younger and served under a guy named—and I am not making this up—Major Redundant, but of course, he didn't spell his last name the same. He spelled it "Rhredondunt," but he had this thick, almost Russian, accent. Anyway, when he said his name, it always sounded like he was saying "Redundant," so we'd all snicker when he said it, and he said his name a lot, usually in the third person, so it was always "Major Redundant likes vodka" or "Major Redundant doesn't want to go back to Chernobyl" or "Major Redundant wants more cabbage soup or some borscht." Anyway, one day, part of our platoon was riding on a T-80 battle tank just outside of Novosibirsk and I had a few extra rubles, so we stopped at a Teremok to pick up a few crepes because we had a long ride coming up to where we would amass on some border of a peaceful East European nation just to scare the bejeezus out of them (ahh, good times, good times). Anyway, so we were on the border of some breakaway republic and I saw this guy waving his arms on the other side of the border, and he was holding up a boxed copy of Lightroom in one hand and a 70¬200mm f/2.8 lens in the other, and he was waving me toward him. I looked over at Major Rhredondunt, and he was busy taking a bribe or chain-smoking or something, and the rest, as they say, is history. Well, made-up history, but history nonetheless. Well, it's like I always say, "Бабушка гадала, надвое сказала."

How Do I... Choose My Paper Size?

In the Print module, click on the Page Setup button at the bottom of the left side Panels area. When the Page Setup dialog appears (shown above; this is the Mac version), choose your Paper Size from one of the presets in the pop-up menu (here, I chose the standard US Letter size, 8.5x11", with borderless [edge-to-edge] printing). That's it—pick one of the preset paper sizes and click OK.

You see that menu on the previous page? The one where you chose your paper size? Yeah, that one. At the bottom of that menu is **Manage Custom Sizes** (on a PC, you may need to click on Properties in the Page Setup dialog, then choose **Custom** to get the Custom Paper Size dialog). Choose that and it brings up the dialog you see above. To enter a size that didn't appear in the preset menu on the previous page, just type in the size you want up in the Width and Height fields. While you're there, in the fields marked Top, Left, Right, and Bottom, you can enter any page margins you want, or just type in "0 in" (like I did here) if you want the image to print all the way to the edges (provided, of course, you have a printer that has the edge-to-edge printing feature but, luckily, most photo printers today seem to have that feature).

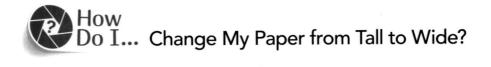

Page Setup

Format For: Canon PRO-1000 series

Canon PRO-1000 series

Paper Size: US Letter Borderless

8.50 by 11.00 inches

Orientation:

Scale: 100%

?   Cancel   OK

It seems like, since you can change just about everything else on a page, there should be a button in Lightroom to do this, but actually this choice is made in the printer software instead (but you do start the process in Lightroom). In the Print module, click on the Page Setup button at the bottom of the left side Panels area. When the OS X or Windows Page Setup dialog appears (shown above; this is the Mac OS X version), click the Orientation button for how you want the page to appear (tall [portrait] or wide [landscape]), and then click OK. That's all there is to it.

How Do I... Choose How Many Photos per Page?

There are a couple of different ways, but we'll start with probably the most-used method, which is choosing how many rows/columns of images you want on your page. In the Page Grid section of the Layout panel (in the right side Panels area), if you choose 1 for Rows and 1 for Columns, you get one image (makes sense, right?). If you want more than one image per page, you just increase either the number of rows or columns. For example, if you drag the Rows slider to 3, you will now have a page with three images stacked vertically, one on top of the other. If, instead, you dragged the Columns slider over to 3, you'd have three images side by side. You'll get a single row or column as long as one of those two sliders stays set to 1. If you move both sliders, the math kicks in. For example, if you drag the Rows slider to 3 and the Columns to 3, you've got a page set up for nine photos (3x3). Another way to choose a multi-photo page is to choose one of the pre-made page templates that come with Lightroom Classic—just go to the Template Browser (in the left side Panels area), click on one of the multi-photo presets, and you're good to go.

Once you've decided on how many photos you want on a page, then go over to the Image Settings panel, in the right side Panels area, and turn on the checkbox for Repeat One Photo per Page (as shown above). Now, it fills every photo cell with the same image.

Another way to repeat the same image is to use the Picture Package feature in the Layout Style panel (in the right side Panels area). This does essentially the same thing as we did on the previous page, but it's designed more to maximize printing as many standard-size images as it can fit on one page, kind of like you'd get from a portrait studio or your kid's school portraits, with different size images, ranging from 4x6s to 5x7s to wallet-size. You do this by either:

(a) Choosing one of the preset templates in the Template Browser (in the left side Panels area) that is set up for the Picture Package feature—there are a few multi-photo presets at the top of the list that are perfect examples, like the 1 (4x6), 6 (2x3) preset I chose here, or

(b) Choosing one of the preset templates in the Template Browser and then going over to the Cells panel (in the right side Panels area) and adding sizes by clicking the buttons. After you've added all the sizes you want, click the Auto Layout button below the sizes to have Lightroom arrange the images in the fewest number of pages possible.

How Do I... Create My Own Layout?

When I want to start from scratch and create my own layout, here's what I do: First, I click on the Maximize Size preset in the Template Browser (as seen above on the left) in the left side Panels area. It's kind of a good neutral starting place. Next (and this is really important), click on the Page Setup button at the bottom of the left side Panels area and choose your paper size now. If you wait to do this until later, your layout will be resized to fit and chances are it won't look the same as you just designed it, but you can sidestep that problem by choosing your paper size and orientation now. From there, the rest is easy: just go to the Layout panel (in the right side Panels area) and drag the Margins sliders to move the image where you want it on the page. By default, that template is just a single-image template, but you can make it a multi-image print by moving the Rows and Columns sliders (just below the Margins sliders).

How Do I... Save My New Custom Layout?

If you come up with a layout you really like, you'll want to be able to save that as a template and use it again with just one click, right? Right! Here's how: click on the + (plus sign) button at the top right of the Template Browser (as seen above left), which brings up the New Template dialog (seen above right). Just type in a name, click Create, and now this new template will appear in the User Templates folder at the bottom of the Template Browser.

How Do I... Overlap Images?

The easiest way to do this is to start by choosing a template that already has an image overlaying another. For example, try clicking on the template called "Custom Centered" over in the Template Browser in the left side Panels area (as shown above). That brings up the layout you see above, with two image boxes overlapping a larger image box. If you only want one image overlapping, just click on the one you want to delete and hit the Delete (PC: Backspace) key. You can resize either of the two remaining boxes by just clicking on them and dragging the corners or sides. Once they're positioned where you want, at the sizes you want them, drag-and-drop images into those cells right from the Filmstrip at the bottom. To change the order of the images (which image appears in front of which), Right-click on an image and choose either Send to Back or Send Backwards (Send Backwards moves it back one level at a time, which is handy if you have more than two images. With just two, it doesn't matter). There are also Send Forwards and Send to Front choices, which bring your image forward or to the very top of the stack.

By default, your background color is white, but if you wanted to change it, it's pretty easy. Go to the Page panel (in the right side Panels area), and the first checkbox at the top is Page Background Color. Once you turn on the checkbox, click on the little color swatch to the right of it to bring up the Page Background Color picker (seen above). It puts the most common page background colors (white, black, and shades of gray) across the top, but you can choose any other shade by clicking in the gradient that appears below it. If you want a colorful background, click at the very bottom of the HEX key on the right side and drag upward, and you'll see a full-color gradient appear where the black-and-white one was. Now, just pick the color you want from the gradient area. When you're done, you can close the color picker by clicking on the little round X in its top-left corner.

This sounds like something that should be super-easy, but it actually takes a few steps (and a little jumping through hoops), but it does work. Basically, you're going to import your logo as an Identity Plate and make it visible on the page. Start by going to the Page panel, in the right side Panels area, and turning on the Identity Plate check-box. Next, click on the down-facing triangle in the bottom right of the Identity Plate preview and choose **Edit** from the pop-up menu to bring up the Identity Plate Editor (seen above). Click on the Use a Graphical Identity Plate radio button, then click the Locate File button, find your logo on your computer, and then click OK to import it (that's what I did above, but the shape of my logo doesn't allow it to fully appear in the long, thin, horizontal preview area, which is about useless in that shape, but don't get me started). Anyway, once you click OK, your logo will appear. You can click-and-drag it where you'd like it, and resize it by clicking-and-dragging one of the corners or using the Scale slider in the Identity Plate section of the Page panel. There's also an Opacity slider there if you want to lower the opacity of your logo (maybe to make it less prevalent). One nice feature is that once you've got this logo imported, you can save it by going back to the Identity Plate Editor, clicking on the pop-up menu in the bottom-left corner that says "Custom," choosing **Save As**, and giving it a name (I named mine Scott's Logo). Now, when I want to add my logo to any print, I don't have to reimport it and stuff—I can just choose it from that pop-up menu in the bottom-right corner of the Identity Plate preview.

How Do I... Add Crop Marks?

If you chose a template (or created a layout from scratch) that has multiple photos in it, and you want to see where to cut the images so they're the proper size, here's how to add crop marks to make the job a lot easier: Go to the Page panel (in the right side Panels area) and turn on the checkbox for Cut Guides. There's a pop-up menu to the right of that, but by default, it is set to Lines, so click on it and choose **Crop Marks**, as shown above on the top right, and it adds crop marks just outside your images, so you'll know where to cut. *Note:* If you choose a single-image layout, this Cut Guides checkbox doesn't appear. Instead, in the Page panel, turn on the Page Options checkbox, and then you'll see a checkbox for Crop Marks. Turn it on (as shown above on the bottom right) and your single image will have crop marks around it.

How Do I... Add Captions under My Images?

I'm going to tell you up front: this is kind of clunky, but it works. Go to the Page panel (in the right side Panels area), and turn on the checkbox for Photo Info. By default, this displays each image's filename under the photo (as seen above). I know what you're thinking: that's not a caption, that's a filename. Right. So, to display a caption, you have to go back to the Library module (press **G**), click on one of the photos you want to add a caption to, then go to the Metadata panel and, in the Caption field (shown above on the left), type in your caption. Yes, you have to do this individually for every photo (don't shoot the messenger). Now, when you go back to the Print module, to the Page panel, to the Photo Info pop-up menu, choose **Caption** (as shown above on the right), and the caption will appear under each photo (well, under each photo you added a caption to, anyway). See what I meant about "clunky" in the first line of this? It works, but it's clunky. Wouldn't it be great if you could just click on each photo in the Print module and type in a caption? Yup, that would be great. If only that worked. Ugh.

Go to the top of the Print Job panel (at the bottom of the right side Panels area), click on the pop-up menu just to the right of Print To (by default, it is set to Printer), and choose **JPEG File**. When you do this, a JPEG Quality slider appears (I use a quality of 80, just in case you care. I think it's a great balance between quality and file size). Also, if you look at what was the Printer button at the bottom right of the right side Panels area, it has changed to Print to File, and that's what you click to save your page layout as a JPEG. That's it.

I'm going to give you a standard method that is very common for online print labs, however the ideal situation is for you to (at the very least) go to the lab's website and see if they have a custom color profile that they prefer. My guess is that they'll tell you to send the files using sRGB color mode (that's the default), but there are labs that have a custom profile, and if they do, you want to download and use theirs to get the best results. That being said, we'll start with the standard method, which is to save the page as a JPEG: go to the Print Job panel, and from the Print To pop-up menu, choose **JPEG File**. Then, down further in the same panel, in the Color Management section, go to Profile and choose **sRGB** from the pop-up menu (as shown above). Now, click the Print to File button at the bottom of the right side Panels area to save your JPEG, with the sRGB color profile for lab printing embedded right into the file. If you downloaded a color profile from your online lab's website, then instead of choosing sRGB from that Profile pop-up menu, you'd choose **Other**, which brings up the Choose Profiles dialog with a list of installed color profiles (shown above on the left), where you choose the profile you installed from the lab. What's nice is that, once you've done this once, that profile will appear in the Profile pop-up menu as a choice from now on, so you don't have to go to that Choose Profiles dialog again. Once your lab's profile is selected, just click the Print to File button to save the file as a JPEG, and you're all set.

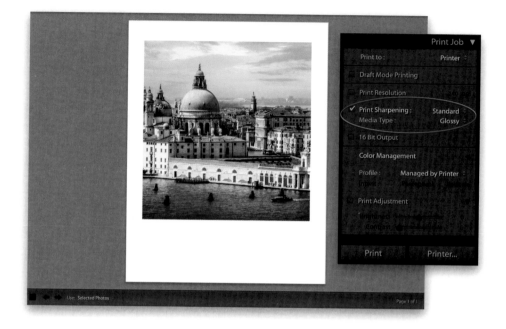

To add print sharpening (yes, we add this even after we've sharpened the image using the sharpening found in the Develop module's Detail panel), just go to the Print Job panel (in the right side Panels area) and turn on the Print Sharpening checkbox. When you do this, you have to tell Lightroom two things: (1) Which type of paper (media) you will be printing on (you make this choice from the Media Type pop-up menu—choose either Glossy or Matte), and (2) the amount of sharpening you want—Low (which is really low), Standard, or High. Then, Lightroom does the math for you, looking at your paper choice, image resolution, and so on, and chooses the proper amount of sharpening for print—it actually does a pretty nice job. The only downside is that it doesn't show you a preview onscreen. You only see the effects of this print sharpening after the image is printed. Just thought you'd want to know.

How Do I... Save My Layout So I Can Print It Again?

If you've created a layout, with the exact photos in the exact order you want them, you can save this layout (so you can go back and print it again any time in the future) by going right above the preview of your image, and on the top right, click on Create Saved Print (shown circled in red above). This brings up the Create Print dialog you see in the inset, where you can name your print, and choose if you'd like it to appear within a collection. There's an option to Include Only Used Photos (which I always turn on because I don't care about photos that aren't in this print, but are now extras). Once you click Create, it adds what looks like a collection to your Collections panel, but the icon for the collection looks like a little printer, so you know it's a print layout. Once you've created this, it remembers not only which photos were in that layout, but the order, so all you have to do to reprint it is click on that collection and you're good to go.

How Do I... Make My Prints as Bright as What I'm Seeing Onscreen?

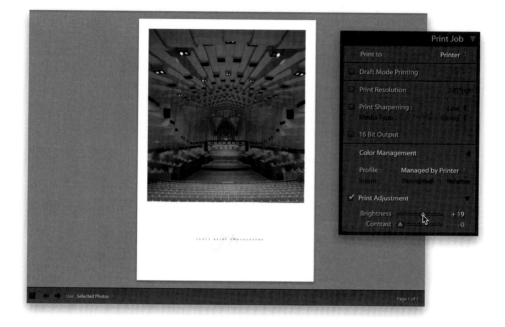

If your prints seem a bit darker than your monitor, that's not unusual. After all, you're looking at a super-bright, backlit, shiny screen, and then printing to non-backlit, not-super-bright, porous paper. In my experience, my prints usually print around 20% or so darker than my monitor. Luckily, there's a way to compensate for this, and make your prints brighter without actually having to adjust the actual image (that way, the image will still look correct onscreen, but just print brighter). You do this in the Print Job panel (in the right side Panels area): at the bottom of the panel, turn on the Print Adjustment checkbox and drag the Brightness slider to the right. Of course, the only way to know how far to drag the Brightness slider is to do a few test prints at different amounts until you find the amount that most closely matches your monitor. The good thing is, once you know that number, you'll just use it every time. There's also a slider for increasing Contrast during the printing process, but you'd only use that if the image not only looks too dark, but also had an overall loss of contrast. Again, you'd have to do a few test prints with different settings to find out how much to increase (or decrease) your Contrast amount. Just remember: when making test prints, you don't have to use large-sized paper—use something like 4x6s, so test prints are cheap and print quickly.

To see an approximation of how your image will look in print (a money-saving feature you can use rather than making a test print) use the Soft Proofing feature. This isn't done in the Print module, though. Instead, select your image, then go to the Develop module and turn on the Soft Proofing checkbox in the toolbar below the center Preview area (if you don't see it, press **Command-T [PC: Ctrl-T]**). Once you turn this on, the gray area behind your image turns solid white (to simulate the look of a print on white paper). Also, if you look below the histogram in the Soft Proofing panel (at the top of the right side Panels area; it says AdobeRGB if it's closed), you'll see the options: choose which printer profile you want to use (from the Profile pop-up menu) and which rendering Intent (Perceptual or Relative), and there's a checkbox to simulate the look of paper and ink. Also, if you want to see if any of the colors in your image are out of the range of what your printer can print (these are called out-of-gamut colors), click on the Destination Gamut Warning in the top-right corner of the histogram (it looks like a tiny page) and any out-of-gamut colors will appear highlighted in red onscreen (fixing out-of-gamut colors is a bit outside the scope of this book, but in short, you can use the Adjustment Brush, painting over the out-of-gamut areas with the Saturation amount lowered, or you can go to the HSL panel, click on the Saturation tab, then get the Targeted Adjustment Tool [it looks like a little target], and click-and-drag downward right over the out-of-gamut areas to desaturate the colors in those areas and bring them into gamut).

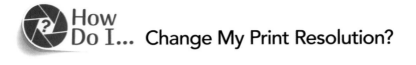

How Do I... Change My Print Resolution?

By default, your image will print at its native resolution (the actual resolution of the image itself), but if for some reason you want to change your resolution (hey, it could happen), go to the Print Job panel (in the right side Panels area), and turn on the Print Resolution checkbox. This makes the resolution field (which is normally grayed out) available, so just click in that field to highlight the amount and type in the resolution figure you'd like, then press the Return (PC: Enter) key to lock in your change.

Ummm...here's the thing: ya don't. Photoshop lets you change its color space, but Lightroom's is preset by Adobe in the ProPhoto RGB color space, so there's no way (or reason) to change Lightroom's native color space. However, you can assign a different color space to images that are leaving Lightroom (you're exporting them as a JPEG or TIFF, etc.). See page 164 in Chapter 7 for assigning a color profile when exporting, or page 228 in this chapter if you're saving a print layout as a JPEG.

If you couldn't find this one easily, it's because Adobe stuck it in an unexpected place—it's in the Image Settings panel in the right side Panels area (I think the panel is misnamed. Maybe "Page Options" or something like that would make more sense, but clearly I'm not on the Lightroom naming committee). Anyway, there you'll find a checkbox for Stroke Border. Once you turn this on, you can choose the color of your stroke by clicking on the color swatch to the far right of the Stroke Border checkbox. You control how thick the border will be using the Width slider.

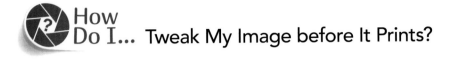

How Do I... Tweak My Image before It Prints?

If you have your image all set in a print layout and you're ready to roll, but you decide you want to change something (white balance, contrast, highlights, whatever), all you have to do is press the letter **D** and it takes your image over to the Develop module, where you can use all the controls there to tweak the image as you'd like. When you're done, press **Command-Option-6 (PC: Ctrl-Alt-6)** to return to the print layout you were last working on.

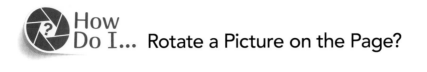

How Do I... Rotate a Picture on the Page?

If you've selected Custom Package (where you can add as many different size cells as you'd like and overlap them) or Picture Package in the Layout Style panel at the top of the right side Panels area, you can rotate an image cell (from wide to tall and vice versa), by Right-clicking anywhere inside its cell and choosing **Rotate Cell** from the pop-up menu that appears. (*Note:* This only rotates the cell, not the image, unless you have the Rotate to Fit checkbox turned on in the Image Settings panel.) If you're using the Single Image/Contact Sheet layout style, you'll need to go to the Layout panel and move the Margins sliders to make a tall or wide layout.

Chapter 11

How to Use Lightroom on Your Mobile Device

It's Lightroom on the Road

If you're thinking, "Hey, I didn't even know you could use Lightroom on your phone," well my friend, you're not alone. Now, depending on the size of your phone, this is either a pretty handy thing, if you have a phone with a big screen, or "You're kidding, right?" if you're still using an iPhone 3 or maybe a Blackberry of some sort, because I don't think that there's a version of Lightroom for the Blackberry, but that's only as I write this, because Adobe is liable to release a Blackberry version at any time. Why would Adobe do this? Well, Blackberry is a Canadian company and everybody knows the Canadians are very good at hockey (I'm not being racist, I'm stereotyping, which is just as bad unless the stereotypical thing you're saying is very positive, like "Canadians are very good at hockey," at which point it simply merges into a compliment, and all Canadians love compliments—see, that's another compliment. Do three of these in a row and it's called a "cat-trick." Sorry, that was a lame hockey pun and my friends from the frozen tundra that is Canada don't deserve that. See? Now that was an unflattering exaggeration because all of Canada is certainly not a frozen tundra, only the areas outside Toronto are frozen tundra, and that's another unflattering exaggeration, but because all Canadians have a great sense of humor, it's totally okay. See what I did there?). Anyway, Adobe is based in San Jose, California, home of the San Jose Sharks hockey team, who play at the SAP Center arena, and you can bet Adobe has some fancy luxury box there, and at some point they'll have to play a Canadian team, probably made up of mostly Blackberry employees, and they don't want things to get awkward between them at the arena, so I think it's probably a lock there will be a Blackberry version of Lightroom sometime in our lifetimes, eh? #gosharks #gotimhortons

The first step is to turn on syncing. So, click on the Lightroom Classic CC logo (in the top-left corner of Lightroom) and, from the pop-up Activity Center menu that appears, click on Sync with Lightroom CC (as seen above on the right). By the way, that's what Lightroom's mobile app is now called—Adobe Lightroom CC. But, I'll probably just call it Lightroom mobile in this chapter, so it doesn't get tedious. Lightroom can only sync collections, not folders, so first make sure the images you want to sync over to Lightroom mobile are in a collection. (*Note:* Adobe no longer calls them "collections" once they hit Lightroom mobile. They call them "albums," so that's what we'll call them here, too.) Once you turn on Sync, you'll see a little box appear to the left of an album's name. Click on that box, and a little sync icon appears (shown circled above in red on the left) to let you know this album is now synced to Lightroom mobile.

In the bottom-right corner of Lightroom mobile's main window, which is called Albums view, you'll see a blue, pill-shaped button. (*Note:* Your synced collections are not called "collections" in Lightroom mobile—they're called "albums" instead.) When you tap on the Add Photos icon (on the left; circled above in red), it takes you to your phone's (or tablet's) Camera Roll, so you can choose which photos to import into Lightroom mobile. Just tap or swipe on any photo to select it (it highlights in blue and a little checkmark appears in the bottom right of the thumbnail to let you know it's selected). When you have all the images selected that you want to import into Lightroom mobile, tap Add Photos at the bottom of the screen and they're imported. You'll now find these images under All Photos—just tap on it at the top of Albums view to see them. If you prefer to import photos from your Camera Roll directly into an existing album, just tap on the album first (in Albums view) and you'll see that blue, pill-shaped button in the bottom-right corner of the album. Tap the Add Photos icon, then tap on **Camera Roll** in the pop-up menu, and it will take you to your phone's (or tablet's) Camera Roll and any photos you import will be added to that album.

The screen you see once Lightroom mobile starts up (kind of its home screen) is called Albums view (shown above left), and it shows a list of any albums (collections) you've synced over from Lightroom Classic, along with any albums you created here from scratch. To see the images inside an album, tap on its thumbnail or its name and you'll see a grid of images (shown above right) similar to what you'd see in Lightroom Classic. To see any image larger (in Loupe view), just tap on it. To return to this Grid view, tap the back arrow icon (circled in red above, on the right image) in the top-left corner. To return to Albums view, tap that back arrow icon again.

How Do I... Change the Size of the Thumbnails in an Album?

Just tap-and-hold two fingers on the screen, and then pinch inward to make your thumbnails smaller (as seen above on the left), or pinch outward to make them larger (as seen above on the right).

How Do I... Create an Album from Scratch?

Just another reminder: collections are called albums here in Lightroom CC for mobile. To create an empty new album from scratch, in Albums view, tap the + (plus sign) icon at the top right of the Albums section, and a pop-up menu appears with choices to create a new album or a new folder. Tap **Create Album** and then give your new album a name (I named mine "portrait shoot," here). To add images to your new album, tap on it in your list of albums, and then once inside, either tap on the Add Photos icon, on the left side of the blue, pill-shaped button in the bottom-right corner of your empty album, and then tap All Photos to add images, or tap on the camera icon to take a photo (using Lightroom mobile's built-in camera app). To delete any album, in Albums view, tap on the three dots to the far right of an album's name, and from the pop-up menu that appears, choose Delete.

Well, first things first—they're called "folders" here in Lightroom mobile, but they work just like the collection sets in Lightroom Classic. To create one, in Albums view, tap the + (plus sign) icon at the top right of the Albums section and a pop-up menu appears (as seen above; on a phone, the menu appears along the bottom of the screen). Your choices here are to create a new album or a new folder. Of course, you'd tap **Create Folder**, and once created, if you go inside that empty folder, you can add more folders (if you want) by tapping the + icon near the top right, or you can put as many albums in there as you'd like. To move an album into a folder, go to Album view, tap the three dots to the far right of an album's name, and choose Move To from the pop-up menu. It will bring up a Destination window with a list of the folders you've created. Tap on the folder you'd like to move it to, then tap Move in the top right. Boom. Done. (Drops the mic.)

How Do I... Hide Everything and Just See My Photo on a Black Background?

Just tap once right on your image, and everything tucks out of sight. To bring everything back, tap once on your image again.

Go to the album that has the image(s) you want to move. In the top-right corner, tap on the three dots, and then tap **Move To** in the pop-up menu that appears. This brings you to the Move To screen (with a blue bar across the top). Tap or swipe over any images you want to move to a different album to select them (they highlight in blue as they're selected), then tap the right-facing arrow in the top-right corner of the screen. This brings you to the Destination screen where you'll tap the check-box next to the album you want to move those selected images into to turn it on, then tap Move up in the top-right corner of the screen. If you want to move your image(s) to an entirely new album, in the Destination screen, tap the + (plus sign) icon near the top right to create a new album or a folder. If you change your mind during the process, tap the X in the top-left corner. Lastly, if you want to keep the image in the same album it's currently in, and instead just make a copy and add it to a different album, then you'd tap **Add To** (instead of Move To).

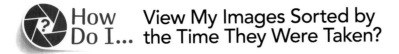

How Do I... View My Images Sorted by the Time They Were Taken?

To change from the standard Grid view for an album (the one we're used to from Lightroom Classic) to a new view that's only found it Lightroom mobile that sorts your images by the time frame of your choice, tap the three dots in the top-right corner of an album. In the pop-up menu that appears, tap on Grid View, then tap on **Segmented**, and now your images are displayed by when they were taken. To change the time frame (from segmented by year, to month, to day, or by the hour, which is what you see above), just tap-and-hold on the date at the top left of a group of images and a pop-up menu will appear where you can make your choice. To return to the regular Flat view grid, tap on the three dots again, tap on Grid View, and then tap on Flat.

The Filmstrip is only available in certain places within Lightroom mobile. For example, on an iPad, when you're in Edit mode, at the bottom right of the screen, just to the left of the round "i" icon (it's above it on an Android tablet), you'll find the Show Filmstrip icon (it's circled above in red; it's a star icon on an Android tablet). Tap that icon to bring up the Filmstrip along the bottom of the screen. You can swipe left/right to move through the images in the Filmstrip, and you can also tap on any image in the Filmstrip to open it in Loupe view. On a phone, it doesn't let you bring up the Filmstrip while you're editing an image, but if you're in Rate & Review mode (tap on the Panels pop-up menu in the top left, to the right of the back arrow icon, then tap on Rate & Review), you can show/hide it by tapping on the three dots in the top-right corner and from the pop-up menu that appears, choosing **Show/Hide Filmstrip**.

How Do I... Reorder Images in an Album?

When you're in an album, tap the three dots in the top-right corner of the screen, and in the pop-up menu that appears, tap on **Sort by Capture Date** (as seen above left. By the way, the red dot you see in some of my images in this chapter is me tapping on a menu command. This is the Show Touches option found under Lightroom mobile's General settings). In the next menu, tap on **Custom** and a little pencil icon will appear to its right (as seen above right). Tap on that icon and it takes you to the Reorder screen (you'll see a blue bar appear across the top of the screen). Now, when you tap-and-hold on a thumbnail a blue outline will appear around that thumbnail, and you can then drag-and-drop it in the order you'd like. When you're done reordering, tap the back arrow icon in the top-left corner. The process is easy and clunky at the same time.

If you want to hand your tablet or phone to someone without having to worry about them accidentally flagging (or unflagging) an image, or messing with anything else for that matter, before you hand them your device, enter Presentation mode. You do this from Grid view by tapping on the three dots in the top-right corner of the screen, and in the pop-up menu that appears, tapping **Present** (as shown above). Or, if you're in Loupe view and want them to see your images starting with a particular image, tap the three dots, then tap **Present from Here**. This hides all the controls, all the Loupe view icons, and most of the interface, so you're safe to hand your tablet or phone over without worrying if they're accidentally going to mess anything up. When they hand it back to you, tap the X icon in the top-left corner.

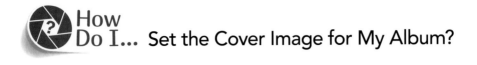

How Do I... Set the Cover Image for My Album?

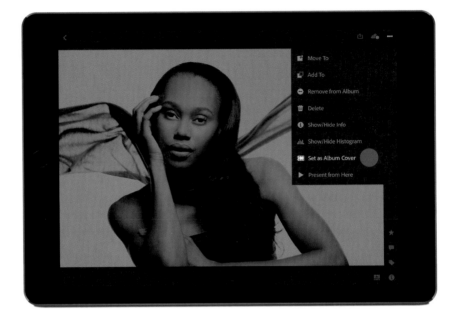

To choose the thumbnail that represents your album (your "cover photo"), first go into an album and tap on the image you want as your cover thumbnail. Then, tap on the three dots in the top-right corner of the screen, and in the pop-up menu that appears, tap **Set as Album Cover** (as seen above). Now that image will appear as the thumbnail for that album.

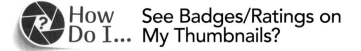

How Do I... See Badges/Ratings on My Thumbnails?

There is actually a lot of info you can display over your thumbnails in Grid view: tap with two fingers to display a badge showing which images are RAW; tap with two fingers again to show any flags and star ratings (as seen above left); tap with two fingers again to display each file's name, pixel dimensions, and the time/date captured; two-finger tap once again to see the EXIF data (f-stop, shutter speed, and ISO; as seen above right); two-finger tap again to show comments and "likes" from a shared gallery (see page 256); and two-finger tap one more time to hide it all from view again.

253

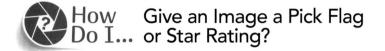

How Do I... Give an Image a Pick Flag or Star Rating?

On an iPad/Android Tablet: Tap on an image to enter Loupe view, then tap the star icon (circled above in red) near the bottom right of the screen to make the flag and star rating icons visible below your image (as seen above). Just tap directly on the Pick or Reject flag, or the star rating you want to assign, or you can use Speed Rating where you swipe up/down on the right side of the screen to assign a flag (a pop-up menu appears in the center of the screen, also seen above) or swipe up/down on the left side of the screen to assign a star rating.

On an iPhone/Android Phone: Tap the Panels pop-up menu in the top-left corner of the screen (to the right of the back arrow icon), and then tap **Rate & Review**. A flag icon will appear on the bottom right and a row of stars on the bottom left. Tap on either one and a menu pops up where you can assign a flag or a star rating. You can also do Speed Rating here by swiping up/down on the right side of the screen to assign a flag or swiping up/down on the left side to assign a star rating (the same menus appear in the center).

How Do I... Just See My Picks or 5-Star Images?

While viewing the images in an album where you've added some Pick flags or star ratings, tap the little funnel-like icon in the top right to bring up a filtering pop-up menu (seen above) where you can choose to see just your Picks or just your Un-flagged or Rejected images. You can also choose to filter by star rating (tap on five, four, three, two, or just one star). If you look at the numbers to the right of these menu choices, it shows you how many images fall into each category. What's cool about this is that you can apply more than one of these filters at the same time. For example, you can tap on Picked and then tap on all five stars to see just your 5-star-rated Picks. To clear any filter, just tap on it again to deselect it. If you decide not to filter by any of these, just tap outside the menu on your thumbnails and it will close the menu.

How Do I... Share an Album with People Online?

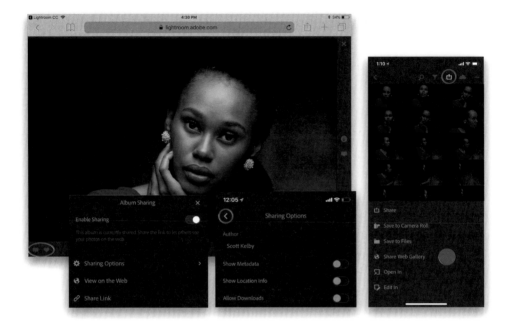

Open the album you want to share online as a web gallery, and then tap the Share icon at the top right of the screen (the square with the upward-facing arrow, circled above on the right). In the pop-up menu that appears, tap on **Share Web Gallery**. This brings up the Album Sharing window where you'll turn on Enable Sharing. Once you've done that, tap on Sharing Options and you'll then choose if you want your metadata included in your images (like your f-stop, ISO, camera make and model), if you want any GPS info included, and if you want people to be able to download your images (maybe you're sharing images from your cousin's wedding or shots from your kid's Little League team, so you want the other parents to be able to download images of their kids). When you're done, tap the back arrow icon in the top left to go back to the Album Sharing window, tap Share Link, and it will bring up your phone's or tablet's Share screen (from your operating system) where you can text that link, email it, or share it directly to social media. By the way, people viewing your gallery can "like" a photo by clicking on the little heart icon and they can also include a comment to you about an image by clicking on the little comment icon (also circled above on the left; they'll need to be signed in with an Adobe ID/ password to do this). Any comments they include are synced back to you and you can see them in that album in Lightroom mobile by tapping on the Comment icon at the top of the screen. You can also see these comments in Lightroom Classic in the Comments panel, at the bottom of the Library module's right side Panels area.

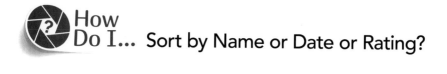

How Do I... Sort by Name or Date or Rating?

When you're in an album, tap on the three dots at the top-right corner of the screen to bring up the Sort menu. Here you can choose to sort by when you took the photo (Capture Date) or the date you imported the images into Lightroom, or the date they were last modified in Lightroom. Tap File Name to sort your images alphabetically and, when you do you, you can change A–Z to Z–A by tapping the sort bar icon on the far right (circled above on the right). Same with tapping Star Rating—you can have 1-star images at the top, or hit that sort bar icon to put 5-star images at the top. The bottom choice (Custom) is for sorting your images manually (see page 250).

Just tap-and-hold anywhere onscreen for a moment to see a Before view of your image with any edits you've made in Lightroom mobile hidden from view. It even says "Before" right at the top of the screen (seen above left), so you know which one you're looking at. When you remove your finger, it returns you to the After view (seen here on the right). Easy peasy.

Tap on the photo to enter Loupe view, then tap on the Edit icon near the top right of the screen (on an iPhone/Android phone, tap the Panels pop-up menu in the top left, then tap on Edit), and then tap on **Color** (its icon looks like a thermometer) to bring out the White Balance options. By default, the WB pop-menu says "As Shot," but if you shot in RAW, when you tap on it, you'll see all the white balance choices you could have chosen in-camera (as shown on the left). If you shot in JPEG or TIFF, your only choices will be Auto and Custom (which means "do-it-yourself manually using the Temp and Tint sliders"). To the right of the WB pop-up menu is the White Balance Selector tool (shown circled above in red on the right). Tap on it and a large loupe appears onscreen, which you can tap-and-drag around your image to try different areas to choose for your white balance. To see a preview of how it looks, release your finger. If it doesn't look right, tap-and-drag it somewhere else, searching for a neutral color, and then take your finger off again. You won't see the adjusted white balance until you remove your finger. When it looks good to you, tap the checkmark icon in the top right of the loupe to set that current color you see on your image as your white balance. Of course, like in Lightroom Classic, you can just drag the Temp and Tint sliders here, too.

How Do I... Tweak How My Image Looks (Develop Module Stuff)?

Tap on an image you want to tweak to enter Loupe view, then:

On an iPad/Android Tablet: Tap on the Edit icon (circled above) near the top right and a set of panels appears, similar to the right side Panels area in Lightroom Classic's Develop module. It's the same sliders, but in a slightly different order.

On an iPhone/Android Phone: Tap the Panels pop-up menu in the top left, then tap on **Edit** and a row of icons appears across the bottom of the screen. If you hold your phone sideways when editing (which I highly recommend), it pretty much looks and feels like Lightroom Classic, with panels on the right side.

In the Light panel, you'll find the sliders that control the tone of your image (Exposure, Whites, Blacks, etc., seen above). The Color panel has White Balance, Vibrance, and Saturation. Effects has Clarity, Dehaze, Vignette, Grain, and a Split Toning button. The Auto button is at the top of the Edits panel, with profiles right below it, along with the Profiles browser. To reset any slider, double-tap on it. For Exposure, Highlights, Whites, Blacks, and Shadows, tap-and-hold *two* fingers anywhere on the slider you're adjusting to see if there's any clipping in the image (the screen will turn black [or white for Shadows/Blacks] and any clipping areas will appear in the color that's clipping or white [black for Shadows/Blacks] if all the colors are clipping in a particular area). At the bottom of the Edits panel is a Reset icon (the downward-facing arrow with a line beneath it) you can tap to undo your adjustments.

Tap on an image you want to crop to enter Loupe view, then:

On an iPad/Android Tablet: Tap on the Crop tool icon (circled above) near the top right and a set of cropping options pops-out.

On an iPhone/Android Phone: Tap the Panels pop-up menu in the top left (to the right of the back arrow icon), then tap on **Edit,** and then tap on the Crop tool icon on the right (or along the bottom if your phone is vertical) and a set of cropping option icons pops out.

Tap the Aspect menu (or the stacked rectangles icon) to bring up a list of built-in cropping presets. To reposition your image within the cropping border, just tap-and-drag it where you want it. The cropping border is locked to the current apsect ratio by default, but if you want to freeform crop, tap the lock icon to unlock it, then tap-and-drag on the sides/top/bottom of the cropping border. There's also a Straighten tool icon you can tap on, and then drag out along an edge in your image (or the horizon line) you want to be straight. When you're finished cropping, tap the Done button (or the checkmark icon) at the bottom right, or if you want to cancel your crop, tap the Cancel button (or the X icon in the top-right corner, if you're wide, or bottom-left corner, if your phone is vertical).

How Do I... Remove Spots or Other Distracting Stuff?

Tap on a photo to enter Loupe view, then tap on the Edit icon near the top right of the screen (on an iPhone/Android phone, tap the Panels pop-up menu in the top left, then tap on Edit), and then tap on **Healing** (its icon looks like a Band-Aid) to bring out the Healing Brush options. First, make the brush slightly larger than the spot you want to remove by using the Size slider on a tablet or by tapping-and-dragging on the Size icon (the third icon down on the left) on a phone (the brush size will appear at the top center of the screen as you drag). Now just tap once on a spot to remove it (as I've done here, where I removed some blemishes). If the thing you want to remove is a power line, or a pole or stick, you'll still make the brush slightly larger, but you'll tap-and-drag over it. A red tint will appear as you drag, so you can see where you're working. When you're done dragging, remove your finger and two selections will appear (as seen here on her hand): one where you dragged (with a blue diamond in the center), and another where Lightroom mobile chose to sample the repair from (with a gray diamond in the center). Fairly often it does a really crappy job of choosing that area, and your repair will look awful, but luckily, you can move that second selection to a better, cleaner, more logical location by tapping on the gray diamond and dragging it to a another spot, and it redoes your removal. To delete any repair, just double-tap on it. The other brush controls, here, are the Feather amount (the softness of the brush's edge) and Opacity.

How Do I... Reset My Edits?

If you just want to start over with your editing (you made some tweaks you don't like, or you just wanted to experiment, etc.):

On an iPad/Android Tablet: Tap the Reset icon (the downward-facing arrow with a line beneath it) at the bottom of the Edits panel.

On an iPhone/Android Phone: Tap the Reset icon (the downward-facing arrow with a line beneath it) at the bottom of the icon panel on the right (if you're holding your phone sideways), or on the right side of the icon panel on the bottom (if you're holding your phone vertically).

This brings up a pop-up menu (seen above) where you can choose: (1) if you want to just reset the adjustments (leaving stuff like any cropping you did still in place); (2) to reset everything (choosing All resets everything, including anything you did to the image in Lightroom Classic on your desktop before you brought it over to Lightroom mobile); (3) to reset To Import, which keeps changes you made in Lightroom Classic, but it resets any changes you made here in Lightroom mobile; or (4) To Open, which will reset it back to when you last opened it.

Tap on an image to see it in Loupe view, then just do a two-finger tap on it (seen marked in red above). Each time you two-finger tap it cycles through a number of different info overlays, similar to what you get with the Lightroom Classic's Info Overlays in Loupe view. The first time you two-finger tap, you get an info readout with the filename, capture time, plus any Pick flags or star ratings. Two-finger tap again and it's replaced with an onscreen histogram at the top left of the image (as seen above). Two-finger tap one last time and the histogram disappears, returning you to your normal view.

Tap on an image you want to apply a preset to, to enter Loupe view, then:

On an iPad/Android Tablet: Tap on the Presets icon (circled above) near the top right to bring up the Presets menu with little thumbnail previews of each preset effect.

On an iPhone/Android Phone: Tap the Panels pop-up menu in the top left (to the right of the back arrow icon), then tap on **Edit**, and then tap on the Presets icon (the two overlapping circles) on the right (or along the bottom if your phone is vertical) and a menu with little thumbnail previews of each preset effect pops out.

To see more sets of presets, on a tablet, just tap on another set, or on a phone, tap on the name of the current set, and a menu will appear where you can access more presets. To apply any preset, just tap on it.

You're going to use the cloud storage–based version of Lightroom, called "Lightroom CC," for the desktop as your syncing app. Don't worry, you don't have to store any images there, or pay a storage fee, or anything like that—you're literally going to use this free Adobe application to simply sync any presets you've bought online, or created yourself in Lightroom Classic (same with creative profiles—ones you've bought or created yourself) over to Lightroom mobile. Here's how I do it: First, find your preset files by going to the Develop module's Presets panel in Lightroom Classic, Right-clicking on any preset you want to sync, and then, from the pop-up menu that appears, choosing **Show in Finder (PC: Show in Explorer)**. Once you see that preset file (it will have ".xmp" at the end of the filename if you're using Lightroom Classic 7.4 or higher), make a new empty folder on your desktop and drag a copy of that preset file into that folder (this will make it easier to find in the next step). Copy as many presets over as you want synced. Then, launch the Lightroom CC desktop application (if you haven't downloaded it yet, go ahead and download it from the Adobe Creative Cloud app). Once you're in Lightroom CC, go under the File menu and choose **Import Profiles & Presets**. In the dialog that appears, navigate to the folder of copied presets you have on your desktop, select all the presets, and click Import. That's it—it imports them into Lightroom CC on your desktop, and just doing that automatically syncs them over to Lightroom mobile—you'll find them at the bottom of the Presets panel, under User Presets.

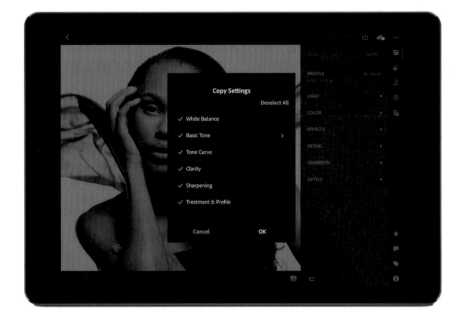

Tap on the image whose settings you want to copy, then tap the three dots in the top-right corner, and in the pop-up menu that appears, tap on **Copy Settings** to bring up the Copy Settings dialog (seen above). By default, just like in Lightroom Classic, it assumes you want to copy everything from this photo and apply it to the next one. If that's indeed what you want to do, then you're all set, bunky— tap OK, swipe over to a different photo, then tap on those three dots again and choose **Paste Settings** from the pop-up menu. If, however, you only want to copy-and-paste some of those settings (let's say you want the tonal stuff, but not the cropping you did to that image), just swipe down the list and turn off the check-box(es) for whatever you don't want (like the Crop checkbox). That way, when you paste, it will paste everything but what you turned off (the cropping). As you swipe down that list, you'll see all sorts of things you can toggle on/off, and near the top right of the dialog is the Deselect All link, which will turn off every setting when tapped (handy if you just want to copy one or two things).

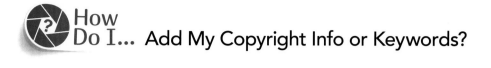

In Albums view, tap the LR icon in the top-left corner to bring up Lightroom mobile's Settings panel. Tap on General and you'll see a list of preferences. If you turn on Add Copyright, the field below becomes active and you can type in your copyright info (i.e., © Scott Kelby 2019. All Rights Reserved.). There are also preferences in the General settings panel for automatically adding photos (anytime you take a photo, even with your phone's regular OS camera app, it gets added to Lightroom mobile automatically). Auto Add Videos does the same thing, but for video (I really didn't need to explain that one, did I?). There's also a toggle switch for whether you want lens profile corrections applied just to RAW photos or all imported photos. Tap the back arrow icon in the top left, and you'll find more settings for everything from cloud storage to a list of gestures you can do inside of Lightroom mobile. To add keywords (search terms), tap on an image to enter Loupe view, then:

On an iPad/Android Tablet: Tap on the Keywords icon (circled above on the right; it looks like a price tag) at the bottom right of the screen, and an Add Keywords field pops out where you can type in keywords.

On an iPhone/Android Phone: Tap the Panels pop-up menu in the top left (to the right of the back arrow icon), then tap on **Keywords**, and now you can type in keywords in the Add Keywords field.

Selfie Flip

File Type

Live Effects

Exposure Lock

Wide to Telephoto

Shutter Button

See the last image

Close camera app

Flash Mode

At the bottom right of Albums view, tap the camera icon on the right side of the blue, pill-shaped button to bring up Lightroom mobile's built-in, kick-butt little camera app. By default, it works like your phone's regular camera app, and images you take with this camera app go into your All Photos album and are synced back to Lightroom Classic automatically. There's a big white shutter button on the right (or on the bottom, if you're holding your phone vertically), and right above/beside it is an icon for switching from the default wide angle to telephoto (more recent iPhones have this two-lens feature, and you'll only see this feature if your phone has two lenses). Next icons up/over: if you want to lock your current exposure, tap the little lock icon and it's locked, and tap the two-overlapping-circles icon for live presets—ones that let you apply a preset look (like B&W or Instagram-like effects) before you even take the shot. On the other side/at the top, there's a "flip the camera, I gotta do a selfie" icon; tap the JPG icon to switch from shooting in the default JPG file format to shooting in RAW (if your phone's camera supports capturing in RAW format. Most iPhones now support shooting in RAW, as do many of the latest Android phones). Lastly, there's an icon for toggling your camera phone's built-in flash on/off. To zoom in, pinch out with two fingers, and to zoom back out again to 100%, pinch in. To close the camera app, tap the X in the bottom-left/top-left corner. This is all pretty basic stuff, but there's more to this camera than meets the eye (as you'll see on the next page).

Controls

Pro Camera
Settings

Switch from
Auto to Pro

Once you're in Lightroom mobile's camera app, below/to the left of the white shutter button it says "Auto." Tap on that and then tap on **Professional** in the pop-up menu. When you do this, Pro mode brings up a bunch of settings you can control, like focus, white balance, ISO, shutter speed, and exposure. Tap on any one of those and either a slider appears (tap-and-drag the slider to adjust the amount) or in this case, where I tapped WB, a list of icons of the various White Balance presets appears. By default, you'll see AWB (Automatic White Balance) is selected, but you can tap on any of the others to change it (Daylight, Cloudy, Fluorescent, Tungsten), or you can tap on the eyedropper to set a custom white balance. When you tap that eyedropper, a square appears in the center of your screen and it says to fill that square with a neutral color. So, find something in your scene that is a light gray, beige, tan, etc., then tap the large checkmark, and it sets that neutral color as your custom white balance. To use the Manual focus, tap the icon with the two brackets and a + (plus sign) in the center. This brings up a slider where you can manually change the focus (areas that are in focus appear with a green highlight on the edges). If you're focusing manually like this, this is a good time to use that two-finger pinch to zoom in—that way you can check your manual focus and makes sure it's good and sharp. Also, in Pro mode, you can tap-and-hold on an area onscreen to lock your focus on that particular spot (you'll see "Focus Locked" appear on the left/at the top of the screen for a second or so). Now you can recompose your shot, and your focus will stay where you locked it.

Access Options

Camera Options Menu

HDR Camera Settings

Switch from Auto to HDR

In Lightroom mobile's camera app, tap on Auto below/to the left of the white shutter button (or Pro, if it says Pro), and then tap on **High Dynamic Range**. This in-camera HDR lets you capture a dynamic tonal range far beyond the camera's normal range. It does this by taking three images at different exposures and then it combines them using the same math as Lightroom Classic (pretty sweet, right?). When you choose to shoot in HDR mode, your individual camera settings are a bit more limited than in Pro mode, but you can still manually set your focus, and choose your white balance and exposure by tapping any one of those icons. Now just take your shot, wait a few seconds while it combines those three exposures into one high dynamic range image, and you're ready to start editing. Also, if you tap the three dots in the top-left/top-right corner, a slew of other cool options pop out over your image area (as seen above where I tapped on the Grid & Level options icon). There are icons for pre-set shooting sizes, from square to 16:9 widescreen; a self timer (from 2 to 10 seconds); different grid overlays and a level feature to help you shoot shots that are straight; and the triangle icon turns on a highlight warning (it shows a zebra stripe effect over blown-out highlight areas). You can do exposure compensation right onscreen any-time by swiping left to make the exposure darker; right to make it brighter. Lastly, there's a gear icon for settings like screen brightness, geotagging photos, and the option to save an uncompressed original RAW, if you're shooting in RAW.

Chapter 12

Other Stuff You'll Want to Know

All That Other Stuff? It's in This Chapter

There are some things in Lightroom that just don't fit into a neat and tidy heading, like troubleshooting for example. Sure, you could make an entire chapter on troubleshooting, but it would be a very, very thin chapter because Lightroom doesn't mess up a whole bunch. Oh, every once in a while you might run into something, but whatever it is, it's not a whole chapter's worth, which left me with this quandary: "Do I leave troubleshooting out of the book altogether, or do I create a nifty little catch-all chapter at the end of the book for all the stuff that has nowhere to go?" Well, you can see from the fact that you are reading this chapter introduction that I went ahead with the plan, but let me tell you, this was not an easy decision, because adding more pages to a book is not something that makes publishers very happy. There was a time when, in the publishing world, the prevailing wisdom was "people want value for their book investment and more pages means more value." I even saw reviews of technology books where the reviewer actually divided the cost of the book by the number of pages in the book to tell you which book was a better value to the reader. Now, this was a flawed way of thinking from the beginning because it supposes that all books on a topic would contain the exact same information presented in exactly the same way, but we know that is not the case because none of the books you could buy on a topic (Lightroom, for example) would dare waste the high cost of paper today (which, by the way, is astronomical) on incredibly silly, quirky, and arguably dumb chapter introductions, except for this book. The value, or lack thereof, of these chapter intros can't be measured with a simple calculator, or even a fancy multi-buttoned Texas Instruments nerdy-guy calculator, because some things are beyond simple measure. So where was I going with all this? I lost me at "hello."

How Do I... Fix Things When Lightroom Starts Acting Weird?

To replace Lightroom's preferences file, first quit Lightroom, then press-and-hold **Option-Shift (PC: Alt-Shift)**, and restart Lightroom. Keep holding those keys down and the dialog you see above will appear. Click the Reset Preferences button and it installs a factory fresh set of preferences for you, and there's a really good chance that whatever problem you were having will be fixed. If the problem persists, I kinda cringe to tell you the next solution, but it's the same one Adobe would tell you if you called their tech support line (of course, this is after they ask, "Have you tried resetting your preferences?"), which is to reinstall Lightroom. If you have to go that route, make sure you've saved any presets or templates you've created (you can usually Right-click directly on them and choose Export from the pop-up menu), but honestly, in most cases you won't have to do the reinstall because resetting the preferences will usually fix the problem.

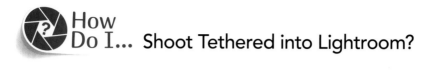

How Do I... Shoot Tethered into Lightroom?

Once your camera is connected to your computer (using the USB cable that came with your camera), go under Lightroom's File menu, under Tethered Capture, and choose **Start Tethered Capture**. This brings up a dialog where you choose where you want these images to be stored, and what to name the folder, and stuff like that. Click OK, and the Tethered Capture "heads-up display" (HUD, seen above) appears. If Lightroom sees your camera, you'll see your camera's name appear on the left side. If it doesn't see it, and you see "No Camera Detected" instead, turn the page and read my Troubleshoot Tethering tips (they will come in handy because Lightroom's tethering is finicky). Once your camera appears in the Tethered Capture HUD, you can hide it from view by pressing **Command-T (PC: Ctrl-T)**. Now when you take a picture, the image will appear in Lightroom (make sure you double-click on the image to make it much larger, or you'll miss out on the main advantage of shooting tethered, which is seeing your images dramatically larger than you would on the tiny 3" LCD screen on the back of your camera). I also press **Shift-Tab** to hide all the panels, so the image is even bigger on my screen. A couple of quick tips: The images come into Lightroom faster if you shoot in JPEG mode, since the file sizes are much smaller (so it takes less time to transfer from the camera to your computer). If you're shooting a Canon camera while you tether, it also writes a copy to your camera's memory card. Nikons don't—the images only go into Lightroom.

How Do I... Troubleshoot Tethering?

Here are five things to try if Lightroom, for some reason or other, either won't tether (of course, make sure that Lightroom actually supports your camera for tethering—check Adobe's list at http://adobe.ly/1dNNjE6) or, more likely, stops tethering at some point in the middle of your shoot (sadly, this is almost guaranteed to happen, which is why you need these five troubleshooting tips): (1) Make sure the camera is on. Press the shutter button to make sure it is awake. If it's awake, just turn it off and then back on. (2) Unplug the USB cable from the camera and then plug it back in, if turning the camera on/off didn't do the trick. (3) Go under Lightroom's File menu, under Tethered Capture, and choose **Stop Tethered Capture**. Then, start the tethering again (from the same menu). (4) If none of those work, try restarting Lightroom. I doubt it'll come to this, but if it still doesn't work, this will usually do the trick. (5) Restart your computer, then launch Lightroom, and turn on tethering. Luckily, numbers 1, 2, or 3 will usually do the trick (in fact, numbers 1 and 2 will probably fix it), but at least you know what to do when it does stop (and it will stop, when you least expect it).

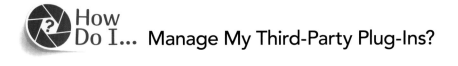

How Do I... Manage My Third-Party Plug-Ins?

Go under the File menu and choose **Plug-in Manager** to bring up the dialog you see above, which is your headquarters for turning on/off plug-ins (including publishing presets to things like Facebook and Flickr), along with a way to add plug-ins (click the Add button below the list on the left). If you want to turn off a plug-in (maybe Lightroom is acting funny and you want to use the process of elimination by turning off plug-ins one by one to see if one of them is causing the problem—hey, it happens), just click on the plug-in you want to turn off (in the list on the left), and then when its options appear on the right, click the Disable button to turn it off.

Click on the image you want to edit in Photoshop and press **Command-E (PC: Ctrl-E)**. If the image is in RAW format, it will open right in Photoshop. If it's a JPEG or a TIFF, the dialog you see above will appear, asking how you want that image to go over to Photoshop. By default, Edit a Copy with Lightroom Adjustments is selected, and I think that's a good, safe way to go (so you're not messing with the original image). In fact, I'd stay away from the Edit Original choice altogether (with one small exception, which I mention on the next page, which only pertains to images you've already edited in Photoshop). The second choice, Edit a Copy is only if you don't want anything you've done to the image in Lightroom to appear in Photoshop. I've never had an occasion to use that option even once—99.9% of the time, I use the top one, I never use the second, and 0.1% of the time, I use the third. Okay, once you've opened an image in Photoshop and edited it there, how do you get it back to Lightroom? Simple. In Photoshop, just Save **(Command-S [PC: Ctrl-S])** and close the image. That's it. Go look back in Lightroom and, right beside your original (or sometimes, for some weird reason, it appears at the bottom of the collection) is your Photoshop-edited file. One more thing: you can choose the name Lightroom automatically assigns to images you take over to Photoshop by going to Lightroom's preferences (under the Lightroom [PC: Edit] menu), clicking on the External Editing tab, and in the File Naming section at the bottom, choosing **Edit** from the pop-up menu, and then creating the filename template you prefer it to use.

When you press **Command-E (PC: Ctrl-E)** to take a layered Photoshop file back over to Photoshop (see previous page), you'll need to choose Edit Original in the dialog you see above, which pops up before your image jumps over there. That's the trick to having the image open with its layers intact in Photoshop. Otherwise, if you choose either of the other two options, the image will open just like it looked in Lightroom, as a flattened image with no layers. So, Lightroom does support layered Photoshop files, but it does it behind the scenes (Lightroom doesn't have a Layers feature, so there's no way to display the layers in that layered Photoshop file). But when you choose Edit Original, then all the layers in that image will now appear when it opens in Photoshop.

When you take an image over to Photoshop, you can send it either as a TIFF or PSD file (and you can choose the color space and bit depth, as well, while you're there). You choose these in Lightroom's Preferences dialog (under the Lightroom [PC: Edit] menu) by clicking on the External Editing tab up top, and then choosing which one you want from the File Format pop-up menu. Personally, I choose PSD format because it keeps all the data fully intact, and because PSD is Photoshop's native file format, the file is dramatically smaller than a TIFF file, without losing any quality. I would say that TIFF is a pretty outdated file format in general, with a big downside of huge file sizes and not much upside, besides the fact that you can open TIFFs in lots of other applications. But, if you're just going to edit the image in Photoshop, why not keep the file size small? You can always choose a different file format to save the image in later, when you export it out of Lightroom, like JPEG or even TIFF at that point, although just for the record, I never save in TIFF format. Ever.

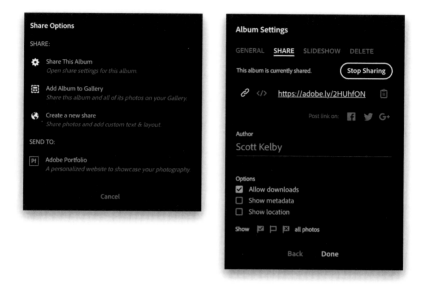

First, turn on Sync (click on the Lightroom logo in the top left and choose Sync with Lightroom CC [that's the mobile app, and you'll need to do this even if you have no plans to use it]). This adds an empty checkbox before each collection's name in the Collections panel, so click the checkbox next to the collection you want to share, and then give it a minute or so to sync. Now, go under the Help menu and choose **View Your Synced Collections on the Web**. This launches your web browser and takes you to lightroom.adobe.com, where you'll log in with your Adobe user ID and password to access your private webpage. Once you log in, you'll see the collection(s) you synced on the left. Click on it to see the images inside, then click Share (near the top center of the window) to bring up the Share Options dialog (seen above left). Choose Share This Album (or one of the other sharing options), and then click the Share this Album button. In the Album Settings dialog (seen above right), click on the clipboard icon to the right of the web address to copy where this collection can be found, so you can email or text it (only people you send this link to will be able to view this collection on the web). If you want this collection shared publicly, so anyone can see it, click the Facebook, Twitter, or Google+ icons to share the link on social media. Near the bottom left, you'll see options for what folks will be able to do when they view your collection on the web. If at any time you want to hide that collection (make it private again), go back to these Album Settings (the same way you got here in the first place), and click the Stop Sharing button.

How Do I... Find All My Virtual Copies?

In the Library module, first go to the Catalog panel in the left side Panels area and click on All Photographs, so we're searching through all your Lightroom images. Then, press the **\[backslash] key** to bring up the Library Filter bar (it appears right above your thumbnails in Grid view) and turn on the Attribute filters. Now, if you look in the bottom-right corner of that bar, you'll see the word "Kind" followed by three icons. Click the center one (as shown circled above) to display nothing but your virtual copies.

Find All My Images That Don't Have My Copyright Added?

In the Library module, go to the Catalog panel, in the left side Panels area, and click on All Photographs, so it searches all the images in your catalog. Now, press the \ [backslash] key if the Library Filter bar isn't visible at the top of your Grid view. From the tabs up at the top, click on Metadata, and then at the top of the first column, click where it says "Date" and choose **Copyright Status** from the pop-up menu. Under that heading, it now shows how many of your images have copyright info embedded (in this case, it was 576 images) and how many don't. Click on Unknown in that list and it brings up all your images that don't have your copyright info embedded (in this case it's 5,550 images). Press **Command-A (PC: Ctrl-A)** to select all these uncopyrighted images. Then, go to the top of the Metadata panel (in the right side Panels area), to the Preset pop-up menu, and choose your copyright preset (as seen here in the inset. See page 4, in Chapter 1, for more on copyright presets). A dialog will appear asking if you want to have your metadata embedded into just the "active" image, or into all of the selected images—click All Selected. Once you apply your metadata to these images, their status is now changed to Copyrighted, and the results of Unknown are now 0 (zero), since there are no longer any images left in your library without your copyright info embedded into them.

How Do I... Make My Color Look Consistent When I Go to Photoshop?

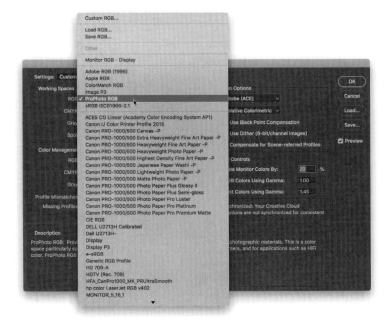

You can't change Lightroom's color space, so you need to change your color space in Photoshop to match Lightroom's default color space of ProPhoto RGB. You do this by going under Photoshop's Edit menu and choosing **Color Settings**. Then, in the Working Spaces section up top, from the RGB pop-up menu, choose **ProPhoto RGB** (as seen above). Also, go to Lightroom's Preferences dialog (under the Light-room [PC: Edit] menu), click on the External Editing tab up top, and make sure, under Edit in Adobe Photoshop, you've chosen ProPhoto RGB for Color Space, so your images will appear in Photoshop in the same color space as you've set up in Photoshop.

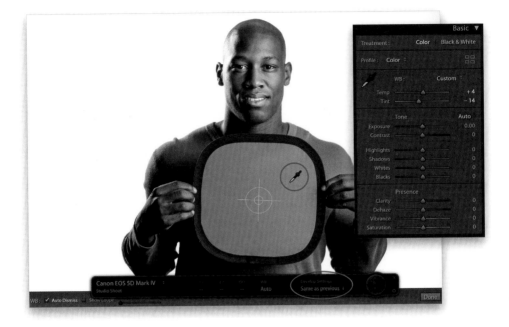

Once your lighting's set, take one shot with a gray card clearly visible in the scene (I like the 12" Lastolite collapsible one for around $40, but use any one you want). Here, we're doing a portrait shoot, so ask your subject to hold it in the center of the frame. There are two ways to do this: one for shooting tethered and one when shooting to your camera's memory card. We'll start with the tethered version: Take one shot with the card in the shot (then your subject can put it down), then take the White Balance Selector tool (from the top left of the Basic panel, in the Develop module's right side Panels area), and click it once directly on the gray card (as shown above) to set your white balance for this shot. Go to the tethering Heads-Up Display (seen above) and, from the Develop Settings pop-up menu, choose **Same as Previous**. Now, when you take another tethered shot, it will automatically have the proper white balance applied to it, because Lightroom will apply to new images the one thing you did to the previous image, which was fix the white balance. If you're not tethering, you still do the same stuff (have them hold the card, etc.), but you can apply the white balance fix after the shoot. Just select *all* your images from that lighting setup, and then click the Sync button switch to turn on Auto Sync (at the bottom of the right side Panels area). Now, go to the shot where your subject's holding the gray card, get the White Balance Selector tool, click on the card, and—boom—all your selected images have that exact same white balance applied. *Tip:* Don't forget to have your subject hold that card again for one shot any time you do a new lighting setup.

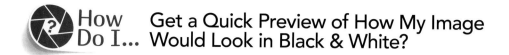

How Do I... Get a Quick Preview of How My Image Would Look in Black & White?

If you're wondering if a certain image would look good in black and white, just press the letter **V** and it shows you the black-and-white version. When you're done, press V to return to the full-color version or, if you fell in love with the black-and-white version, don't press V again and it stays black and white.

It's a simple keyboard shortcut: with the Crop Overlay tool **(R)** active, just press the letter **X** and it toggles back and forth between tall and wide, as seen above.

In the Library module, select the photo you want to convert to DNG, then go under the Library menu up top and choose **Convert Photo to DNG** (as shown above), and that'll do it. You can also choose to convert your images into DNG format when you first import them into Lightroom by clicking on Copy as DNG at the top of the Import window.

How Do I... Edit Video in Lightroom?

I'm not quite sure "edit" a video is the right term. It's more like trim a video, or use a video in a slide show. Here's how: First, you'll be able to see which files are video files because you'll see the length of the video clip in the lower-left corner of their thumbnails in the Library module's Grid view. If you double-click on a thumbnail, it brings up your video in Loupe view, and if you click on the little gear icon (the Trim Video button) at the right end of the control bar below the video, the trim controls pop up (seen above), where you can drag the little handles on either end of the clip inward to where you want the video to start and stop (here, I'm dragging the right end in toward the left to trim off the end of the video). To choose which frame appears as a thumbnail for this clip (think of the frozen screenshot that appears on videos on sites like YouTube), click on the Frame button to the left of the Trim Video button, and choose **Set Poster Frame**.

Index